Life Is So . . . You Know

Deon H. '17

authorHOUSE®

AuthorHouse™
1663 Liberty Drive
Bloomington, IN 47403
www.authorhouse.com
Phone: 1 (800) 839-8640

Published by AuthorHouse 11/20/2017

ISBN: 978-1-5462-0721-4 (sc)
ISBN: 978-1-5462-0719-1 (hc)
ISBN: 978-1-5462-0720-7 (e)

Library of Congress Control Number: 2017913754

Print information available on the last page.

Contents

Opening: Small Book Dream

For the past few years I've envisioned this small book. I mean a really small book. Almost like a pocket dictionary in stature. In my vision, the book is very unassuming to the reader. The cover, not fancy with graphic designs. The cover simply says "Life is so.... You Know" That's it!

I use to bring it up to my wife every now and then to hear her response. Her response, "ohhh okay..... small like what?" Her expression saying silently "what are you talking about?" Then I'd get real hype and be like, "baby, a real small book with a lot of stuff in it!" I'm trying to sell it like lemonade, but she dead pans, "stuff like what?" I respond in exuberant confidence – "LIFE STUFF!"

You feel me don't you? Alright you're not feeling me - but it's still my vision! As a matter of fact, vision accomplished because you're reading it now. Life is so......you know. That's not convoluted or hard to catch, is it? Life is so....

My vision so clear to me: A small book with no more than 9-10 chapters of real life topics. Intentionally small so that I can't swash buckle you to death with wasted words. Instead, my small book would give you more punch! Was that a good way to phrase it? Or how about, "more bang for your buck?"

A small book dealing with issues about life. - Your life, my life, good life, bad life, and all that life brings. Each chapter extremely small so that my words have to matter. Do you kind of feel me now? Maybe you don't understand, but by reading the opening - it worked! Yes!

Forgive me for getting excited, let me get back to the small book. I figured I better do it now before my wits decrepitude.

So look, the book has me, a regular dude talking about real LIFE $***! No egocentric author, scholar, doctor, or know it all expert. This way you can get a different spin on issues you ponder every day. Who am I??? Just a guy with a lot on his mind, depending on the small book to let me get them off! See how I keep stressing "small book."

I will talk about God, life, love, politics, marriage, entertainment, race, hate, and so much more. I'm not touching the cookie cutter topics - too easy. I want to earn your money not be fallacious with this small book. How did that sound for an infomercial? Would you buy it? Tell the truth.

Ok, let me be serious for a moment....The small book is going to simplify issues for you. It's going to motivate you and captivate your emotions. It will give you hope, in a hopeless appearing world. I will give you a voice. I will also provoke you.

The small book is yours. It's with you in times of happiness or sadness. I am not starting out on this endeavor to gain acclaim. If a Pulitzer comes for this work - I will donate it. Excuse my humility but that will be the running joke throughout the book. (Pulitzer for the small book) - The nerve of me.....

But in all seriousness, a lot can be accomplished inside this short work. Maybe you will find healing; whatever the case may be thank you for your support.

Whether you are in Chicago, Atlanta, Houston, or Detroit, I feel you. Vallejo (Yayo), Boston, Denver, and Mobile. I know we are all living this life together.

What's up Yonkers, Portsmouth, Jackson Miss., and Cleveland. Charlotte, Charm City, Nashville (The Boss), Compton, and Pittsburgh. OKC, New Orleans, Phoenix, Miami (pork n' beans), Philly, Seattle, Dallas, Maryland, and St. Louie. Can't forget Indianapolis, Omaha, Salt Lake, Little Rock, Wichita, Toronto, Richmond, Jersey, and The Cap. (Ovechkin).

Man I got quite a few more spots to shout out, but it's a small book. I got you next time. Gotta get the preachers, singers, actors, teachers, trappers, rappers, wives, husbands, churches, colleges, frats, doctors, and lawyers. To the writers, planners, hustlers, caretakers and dreamers. To all people, rich or poor, hopeful or pessimistic. I'm here.

Speeding up...... I can't have no long drawn out opening and be marketing this the small book. That might mess up my marketing strategy. At least you do know I have a strategy. So may God bless you and please enjoy

"Life is so....You Know" Thanks.

"A special prayer to the people in the city of Houston. As you Rebuild your home's, and your lives believe ; in God's purpose for you."

1

Truth

We search for truth, but often times find a lie. Some of us will risk life and limb for 20 minutes of fame. People are lost inside of cell phone screens and reality T.V. dreams. Donald Trump did it - so can I! Hold on a second, let me check my Twitter. Oh you foolish souls...... I am here to save you from your sleeping stupor. No need to thank me, our world depends on it. Not on me - you! This is the ninth inning and we already got two outs. You are on deck. You said "put me in coach!" Our team needs you. Narrow your focus, wake up and seek truth.

When Donald Trump won. I WAS LIVID! (real mad homie). Maybe it was the decades' long decay of democrat distorting me. Or maybe the delusional lust I have with history being made. I don't know, but I was upset. How did he arrive so fast without the gradient process usually taken?

When I woke up the next morning, the facts literally felt like a dream. Sad to say - no dream at all!

This small, short piece of literature is for all of you who are tired of tongue twisters, bull shitters, and all the other listers who lie. Not lies in the literal sense of lie, but the lie of covering up what we feel......what we know (even worse).

For instance, I am not a heavy curser.

But in this small book I will let it come out as it chooses (sorry ma). With that said, I was mad as hell when Trump won! Not that I was hating on Trump (quietly I was), but it felt like he fooled 50 million people, and it was nothing I could do about it! Anger at my core screaming out for attention but no one would listen.

"How did we get here?" my cynical mind wondered....

How could 50 million people not see the dupe in motion? Was all of us green as a pool table? - unable to see the short con - conning us into submission? Well I guess that's the AmeriCON way (take – trick - bamboozle). Former New York City Mayor Michael Bloomberg, even called Trump a con.

Look, this is not gonna be some long drawn out book of B.S. to trick you out of your hard earned cash. Why would I be so AmeriCon to you? Let me clear something up real quick also.... This is not an anti – American - I hate politics piece either. This shit is just REAL!

I want it short for a reason. We like things short right? The new found idea of simple America is but a forgone conclusion of rubbish. Quick and to the point right? You are not getting a bunch of mystery and intrigue (not Grisham). This is also not a help yourself book. If you want to lose weight - it's simple:

#1 Eat natural foods (preferably green)

#2 Drink water at least 5xs a day

#3 Move, Walk, Run, (limit sugar)

That's it - now lose some weight!

Hate to make what is so hard to many, sound so easy but in a weird way it is. Your mind has the ability to overcome anything! I have an idea.....

Mentally compare losing 20 pounds to Donald Trump becoming president. If Trump believed he could be president - you can believe you can lose 20 pounds! You feel me?

Seriously, you can do it if you simply stop thinking of reasons why you can't. Can't is not okay? It's all a matter of mind conditioning. You can condition your mind to do anything you want it to do - it's yours. This is truth....

My wife and I had this grand plan to be vendors at the inauguration (actually my plan). This was when Hillary was running hard. The Donald was being accused of all kinds of things including grabbing women by there you know what. We were counting the cash in our heads - ching ching. Money has a way of tunneling your vision. We started ordering hats, buttons, Madame President memorabilia. You name it. As I said, it was my idea - so I'm feeling like a damn genius! Gloating in my brilliance......

All we had to do was go down to the courthouse get a police clearance, vendors license, and we good. Then suddenly, the news started to change...... Hillary had more leaked emails, and something else about weird ass Anthony Weiner. How the hell is Anthony Weiner affecting Hillary's chances at winning? I was confused, and so was my wife. So we stopped buying things and followed the ever evolving joke of our democracy. I thought to myself, "the world must be laughing."

Saturday night live was killing the game with Alec Baldwin (Trump) and Kate McKinnon (Hillary) delivering insane sketches. But as we all laughed, the silent joke was on us. From the green lush hills of Scotland, to the tiny shacks of Haiti, the world was laughing at us!

That's another reason why this will be short...... enough has already been said. In my opinion, people talk too much anyway without really saying much. Did the great founders of our country waste words so cantankerously?

My wife and I still had hope though. CNN had Hillary up 6-8 points, as well as other news outlets. So, wifey and I were back counting the dough, (ching ching). I even had quiet moments where I reflected on the immense historical ramifications this would have on America. I thought about my daughters, and the world changing before their eyes.

The thought of little girls from southeast D.C. to Vallejo California, now believing that anything was possible. The glass ceiling really broken!

Then on that foggy night, inside of living rooms everywhere, the unthinkable happened.....Trump had an early lead. No big deal said George Stephanopoulos and other pundits - "the night is early." What's the saying, "the turtle catches up eventually?"

Well on this night, one of my other sayings was more appropriate... "Ain't no fun when the rabbit got the gun?" Trump was the rabbit and he was holding the gun to the other 50 million of us who thought HELL NO!

The women of the view were on lifetime in hysteria! The live crowd on B.E.T. stunned. Let's not forget the pundits, still rationalizing the math.

Well if Michigan does this, or Pennsylvania does that, Hillary will be all good. It honestly felt like the world stood still, turning on its indelible axis in mockery of such a night.

Time stood still laughing at us. My wife slept comfortably, almost assured of waking up to her first female president in her 45 years of life. If she only knew what was unfolding before my very eyes.

As the night stumbled on, things became increasingly obvious. To even optimist among us, Donald J. Trump would be the next President of the United States of America.

Live look-ins at Hillary's presumptive victory party were heart wrenching. To see the many supporters, donors, and volunteers (mostly young women) crying in despair was tough. On the other side was the Trump party; arrogant in their smell stench of success on display. I knew damn well a lot of them were just as surprised as the other 50 million of us Hillary supporters - shock and awe!

They played it off though. Fake it 'til you make it.

Regardless of which, it was all a mess. The rabbit had the gun and he was laughing at us. I was in bed before Trumps acceptance speech. Sleep hardly an option. So I laid there in my colder than normal spot of the bed, envisioning that brash smile and "I told you so" look etched across Trumps face.

Let me clarify something.....I do not hate Trump. It's not even about him for real.

It's about US against *THEM*; and *them* had won again! But this time - them had done it in the most unusual fashion. Sneaking through some unsuspecting backdoor, like a speakeasy for Chicago gangsters. *Them* did it with a 2016 version of the great white hope! Buster Douglas beating Tyson. They got us good this time. It hurts to even write about it. Trumped!

"*We*" are the disenfranchised that have held the smaller cup for all of our lives. "*We*" never had the privilege of private schools or manicured lawns to wake up to. There was no abundance of choice steaks and chilled refreshments for *we*. "*We*" are the 9 to 5er's that cling to jaded hopes and dreams of a fair America. Maybe it is bullshit - but you sold it to us and we bought it! So let me get to the real reason why, it hurts so bad.

Not only did Trump win, he did it with a lot of "*WE*". Somehow, he convinced a lot of *we* that he was for us. He rallied in Florida, Ohio, and even in Michigan. (come on Detroit) I guess we had grown tired of the broken promises. He came to we and enough of us turned out for him to win.

The exit polls say it was rural white men who came out in record numbers for Trump. It was way more than that! It was also the Black, White, and

Hispanic inner city voters who didn't come out. So us not coming out, won it for Trump.

This should be the part where I blame Hillary for what she did or did not do. It would be easy, but why waste the verbiage on such fickle rhetoric.

Hillary will have the rest of her life to sit on the back deck of her sprawling estate with Bill and conjure how the rabbit got the gun. Besides, I love Hillary. She has been a soldier throughout her life. A public servant, wife, mother, and woman.

Did she make mistakes? Of course! Did she deny the release of her tax returns, insult women, Mexicans, and the disabled? No. So keeping this all the way real with you, Hillary is not as bad as people make her out to be. I honestly believe she had great intentions with bad baggage in tow. I also pray she finds peace in what had to be a devastating night.

So let's speed up a few months to this Trump presidency.... People are still in the streets protesting. Is the immigration crack down fair? - The travel ban on Muslim territories? Why is Trump so fixated on

President Obama with all the, he tapped the phones at Trump tower blah... blah.....blah....... Never has so much happened in the first 100 days of a president in history.

Attorney General Jeff Sessions alleged communication with the Russians (oh yeah Russia); the strange selection of his cabinet, or belief by many that Bannon is the real string puller behind the puppet. Trump has stated very emphatically during the campaign "I'm no puppet." So, what's true - what's false?

Fake news alert stupid Americans! Could Russia really hack an American election?

Of course they can, we are talking about Russia duh!!!! But for now, be lucky you got me..... Some guy sitting God knows where, typing on this little apparatus, trying to make sense out of a world that offers many questions and not enough answers.....

I still believe that we are more alike than different.

The media feeds us this perception that we are divided by race, class, and politics. When in reality, we are only divided by truth! Some of us were told the truth, and some of us were lied to. Real talk!

If you were taught to hate fat people - you were lied to. You do not have to hate anyone. But we live in a world where ideals are catered by our fears and premonitions.

Black men are violent drug dealers; police are aggressive and abusive; rich people are greedy." There's no way each member of a class is identical in nature or deed. Be for real!

So as fate would have it, my wife and I sucked up the Hillary memorabilia as a loss! (election over) We then had the nerve to invest in Trump stuff (don't laugh). As much as we disagreed with his victory, we clung to the adage of Making America Great Again! Trump items in tow, we'd try vending at the inauguration.

Guess what happened??? Nothing is how my wife would describe it. A day of vending in our nations inaugural event was sieged with anger, riots, and frustration. (people were trippin) After just a few hours, my wife thought it best to pack up for safety and cut our losses! We were only trying to offer our piece to making it great again, but no one cared.

Our beliefs have distorted our humanity so much, that winning and losing carries far more referendum than thought or principal.

Do I agree that he won - hell no! But can we circumvent hate our way to peace? Can we simplify the anger of 50 million people, with vilifying one man? The answer is no!

We must become educated about who we are and why we are. Why are we so mad about Donald Trump and all of his antics, yet sleeping well through the chilling murders of children in Chicago? We cry tears as our musicians sing or sports stars score, but remain silent as our teachers are underpaid. Is this too much for you???? Would you rather close this small book now and spare yourself the self-introspect of what such piercing words bring?

You CAN lose that 20 pounds. You CAN revolutionize Hillary's defeat. I do not hate Donald Trump, I just disagree with his ideals. So my contribution are these words - my truth! Its only 9 chapters for a reason..... It's pain.... It's 2017.... It's US!

2017 is unlike any other year in history. So many issues are unresolved. A Trump presidency reeling with scandal and fake news accusations. Is it fake news because he disagrees with its message?

We all must sit and wonder what's next on the horizon. Just when you thought you'd seen it all, another level of "I can't believe that happened" happens. Hold on to your seats cause it's gonna be a wild ride!

Here's the latest on President Trump.... Trump and Kim Jong are beefing. It's all about big bombs, and big egos. Why do we have nuclear missiles, but reject anyone else from having them? President Trump is also feuding with Canada over trade. Then you've got that HUGE wall he intends to build with your tax dollars. Billions!

The political landscape is in transition. President Obama recently made his first public appearance since leaving office.

His primary mission is inspiring future political leaders. Of course that's code talk for "rallying the troops against Trump!" The plot thickens for 2020.

As I mentioned earlier, educate yourself! Educate yourself to things you hate or dislike. The education will help you understand those things better. Take a moment away from your stuffy ass reality, and see what someone else's reality is. Yeah, I'm talking to you!

I use to have a serious problem with the well-heeled among us. People who kind of slid into money. Those who were born into privilege. But one day I had to be honest with myself..... Would I not want the very thing I take issue with? Who really wants to work hard as hell all their lives to die owning a Cadillac? So parts of me were envious, and other parts were jealous. I had to grow up.

When I put both of those worthless sentiments aside and started educating myself about money, it became clear that it's available to all of us! Some people just get a head start. It's not their fault - the cards are dealt. So educate yourself about your fears.

Stop being so stuck on you! Understand why a person may feel more comfortable living as another gender. Losing weight may be harder for you than your co-worker. We are all different in our own way. Stop judging what you don't understand. To know 2017 is to know what you're dealing with. To know what you're dealing with, is to know your fears.

Maybe your fear of love, is because your parents' marriage ended in divorce. Maybe your fear of black men is the evening news exploitation of them. Our perceptions keep us trapped in a bottle without a panoramic view.

And if we can't see all angles, we have no true options. To feel different - you must see different!

I am reaching out to you wherever you may be in life. If you are in a good place, I am happy for you. If you are not in such a good place, I'm here with you. I feel your pain. In my life many challenges have come to me without solutions. We call that on the job training! We are left to fix things with no real guide. But if you stop and think however, you will see that you have the capabilities. You are an over comer - resilient!

The election may have had a profound effect on you. Some people have admitted bouts of anxiety and even depression. Know this - you have a say. Your hope speaks by the actions you take, counter to the issues that confront you in life. Learn the process of government. Learn about the midterm elections and local elections. Those are far more vital to your day to day life. Governors, Congress, Senate, Alderman's, Mayors, and city council members are critical to your everyday life. That's where inches are fought for!

Let me get ready to wrap this first chapter up. This is my first problem with the small book - there's so much more to be said. But it's the small book, I must show restraint. *Life is so.... you know.* You do know don't you? Man it's a lot. Stay with me though - it gets deeper.....

Quote me.

I'm not seeking the truth nor was I ever. I was born knowing the truth. Everybody is. Trouble is they get it knocked out of them before they can walk.

- Bob Dylan

2

God Must Be Laughing

Have you ever tried to laugh something off? Like someone tells you something, or you hear something and try to play it off? Have you ever laughed to keep from crying? I have, and I can imagine God up there doing the same thing. To see all corners of the world in conflict. The wars, the poverty, the desensitization of humanity. The rebirth of Sodom and Gomorrah. Was that too dark? When's the last time you watched your local and world news? I watched it yesterday. Maybe I could have used a better example than Sodom. Give me one. As a matter of fact, never mind....... Give me a prayer instead. After you pray - give it to God. Don't mind if it appears that God is laughing. Your prayer will be taken seriously. Sometimes we laugh to keep from crying.

For those of us who believe in God, can you imagine what he's doing up there? My opinion He's probably crying tears of sorrow. I can imagine God weeping for the war in the Middle East. To see the world in such chaos, must put a strain on God. We are all His children, and the pain a parent feels for a helpless child is hard.

Why has religion caused more pain than any other factor in history?

Allah, has almost turned into a bad word. Where in Arabic language - it means God? So why does the word Allah inflict such fear? Then again, God must be laughing to keep from crying.

All of my life, I've been confused about the turmoil with Israel and Palestine. The Gaza strip, etc... etc.... etc.....Like, who goes to war on Holy land? And why is religion short on compassion?

When I finally did the research and found out it was about land and beliefs, I was even more confused. Like where in the Qur'an, or Bible, does it say to kill? How are people actually okay with this? What kind of life exists in a war zone?

For some people in the Middle East, it's an everyday reality. Clubs are being shot up, and cafes are bombed. In Syria, chemical warfare is administered without warning. Peace all but a fleeting memory.

As a child, my mother would wake me up on Sunday mornings with gospel music playing. The waft of bacon filling the open air of our tiny apartment. Mama putting on one of those front pew ready church dresses. I'm trying to duck church - but mama's persistent. She believed that church was a cornerstone to change.

Our apartment was across the street from a 21 hour a day liquor store. Bass liquors sat on the Maryland /D.C. line. Rhode Island and Eastern avenues to be exact. My young mind use to wonder, "how can people drink that much?"

A drunk named Blue use to sleep in our hallway. We stayed on the third floor and Blue would always sleep by our door. Bushy hair and scruffy beard. Mama would chase Blue off, and then throw pneumonia down to get rid of the wine smell.

The Sunday rides to church were always quiet. It was like the city had a Sunday peace treaty on noise and violence.

I can even remember Sundays in Baltimore being the same. Peace, tranquility, and a break from gunshots.

Our church was St. Paul's Baptist. A small, family oriented place of worship. I spent most Sundays running the halls, and sneaking to the 7 eleven with

Butchie Maxwell. Butchie was my childhood partner in crime. Our capers consisting of conning Mrs. Maxwell, (Butchie's mom) out of candy.

Whenever in church, I always felt something! If the choir sang, or Reverend Williams preached, something inside me moved. Mama would always say "that's the spirit moving".

I knew without question then, as I know now, that God is real! These days it's almost taboo to talk openly about God or faith. Too much sensitivity (Ralph Tresvant). Why is it so wrong for someone to announce faith in public forums? As if not to offend anybody. - Seriously?

Should I be offended by two men kissing at a stop light? Or by a woman in her 50's, still wearing tight skirts and 6 inch heels? This is not a declaration of homophobia, or hating on the 50 year old woman. She might still got it! My point is, how did the world become so religiously intolerant?

If I love God - so what! Why are you in my business? I just find it strange that we are quick to believe that technology is the greatest thing ever but God???

We praise Apple, Facebook, and Twitter. Say God, and it gets quiet. Weird.....

Let's go back to the Middle East... What the hell is going on over there? Imagine the kids waking up to that reality every day.

How about that for third grade reality? And the culprits have the nerve to justify it with religion. Nah dog! You cannot defame the name of God with anger, hate, demagoguery, murder, or torture!

And why are people calling these sects of hate, religious groups? There's no political or symbolic reason to say 'Islamic extremists.' If they're prevocating evil than it's not Islam.

"Extreme" or "radical" cannot be in the company of God. So why does the government and media sync the two together? It's all propaganda.

I can still remember the day that my daughter told me she wanted to be Muslim. I pondered a response in the solitude of my thoughts. I responded how a father who loves his daughter should. I told her to study and research exactly what she was about to embrace from all angles. That means, not only as a believer in Islam, but also as a future wife, mother, and woman. That was about 6 years ago.

My daughter is now married to a good man, who happens to be Muslim. She herself has been a Muslim for over 5 years now. I love her unconditionally.

God means so much in my day to day life.

I'm already dysfunctional enough, so if you took Gods mercy from me - where would I be? Let me tell you where I'd be: I would be a lost, 40 something year old man, thinking I had it together. Faking it! God gives me the balance that I would scarcely lack if I was doing life on my own. I'm not that good!

By me giving you my truth, it allows you into my spiritual sanctum. It's me questioning with you, "why has religion been the catalyst of so many wars over time?" If religion is so good for us, why has it been so bad for the world?

That's why God must be crying... Because how could we get this simple merger of life so wrong? Acknowledge God -and your life is better. Simple.

How did we get from the great prophets to here? Some of the greatest to ever walk earth like Jesus, Gandhi, and Mohammed, all looked to God. There was no greatness without him! Now, we take all the credit. We got it all together. We are great on our own merit, and not because of something greater than us? Tweet that!

All of this is uncomplicated right? Than why is nobody talking about it? It feels like we're all eluding each other for some reason. The only person I can have this conversation with is my wife. She shares my sentiment on the lack of tolerance we have as people for God. She also shares my truth on where she'd be without him.

It's not hard to sit down and really decipher what indifference we should have against the messengers of our lives. People feed us garbage - and we keep eating it up! No refusal offered.

Look at how school shootings are but a footnote now. "Newsbreak - six teens shot at Pennsylvania school, story live at 5." Live at 5??? - What the hell are you talking about? Six teens got shot in a school, and you want me to wait until 5 for the details? Be for real! Less God has only equated to more hate.

Let me clear something up..... I am not pushing God or religion at you. Whether you believe in God or not, that's your call! My truth consists that if God was more based in our life culture, things would be better. Because with a moral compass, comes moral responsibility. So it's on the pundits or critics to prove my truth wrong! I will die with this belief.

You are so out of touch, and you know that something is missing. You just don't know how to get to it. Is that you? If you are reading this now, and you feel an emptiness inside of you and you don't know what to do - just pray. Just say "God, if You are real and I am Your child, than please reveal Yourself to me." Just say that and mean it. I guarantee He will show Himself to you in HIS way. It may not be a loud boom of thunder or vivid dream, but you will know.

You see, God doesn't have to show Himself to you. -I'm God, should I have to prove Myself to you? Who are you, but 1 of 6 billion people living on Earth? Why should I have to prove myself? I should be evident in the movements of the wind or motion of the oceans. The evidence of Me is on display every day for all eyes to see.

Why would something so great be in pride to please you? Only the insecure human would try to prove a point - not God! God just is...

I don't care what anyone feels about this chapter.

My expression of self to you is about my love for God. It's not up for debate! If I should win a Pulitzer for this work, I will offer no comment. The award will never grace the mantle of my home, or be the token of hubris I should need in my old age to keep my ego erect. I don't want it! Donate it to the most down trodden elementary school you can find. For the inspiration that God has given me should not be rewarded.

Winston Churchill once said that - "men occasionally stumble over the truth, but most of them pick themselves up and hurry off as if nothing had happened".

That's deep! To know something for yourself, but consciously suppress it out of fear. We do it all the time as people. We will hear something said of enormous power and profoundness, but never pass it on. Why is that? If you had a morsel of truth that could edify ones being one iota, is it only right to share it?

Well, welcome to Life is so....you know. I am telling you now that God is real, and his works and miracles are effervescent every day! The brilliant minds of Emerson, Shakespeare, Nietzsche, Einstein, Earhart, Mandela, Wilde and others were all inspired. Who made them great? What made them great? Is greatness a gift or quest? Can you even pursue the quest without the desired gift?

Many would argue that we make ourselves great through passion, preparation and opportunity. I say today, right here, right now, that God alone makes greatness! If not, we would all be great.....

God knows your life's course before you enter the world. All of the intricate parts of you are designed. It says in the bible that a 1,000 days is like 1 day in the eyes of God. So if I had such exponential foresight of life, how could I not know what was needed at any precise time?

Look at history and you be the judge. When something was needed to push humanity further, the right person was always available. They were already born to be useful, for that destine moment in time. Whether it be Ford, The Wright Brothers, Carnegie, J.P. Morgan, or even Harriet

Tubman. These people came along at calculated moments. God given moments! By design.

Yes, they seized the moments, but God created each moment to be seized.

I knew there was no way I could go past the first two chapters without addressing the most important truth in my life. It not only honors God, but it's a compliment to my mother, who planted the seed inside of me.

I have always wondered how scientists, with their big bang and evolution theories, could miss the obvious. Who made it bang? Who made it evolve? Can any act of progress, proceed without a process? Want that in slang? .... Can things just happen without something making it happen? Of course not!

If there's nothing else that I know to be true, it's that God is real! So how do we accept diabolical acts portrayed as killing in the name of God? It's no time to be silent as innocent people are being stolen by hate every day. Then for Donald Trump to wage war on religion by pigeonholing some into one - is also wrong! Hate is not conditioned by ideals, more so than it is by the heart.

Which brings me back to my original statement..... God must be crying. Because the state of religion has twisted into a hyperbole of inaccuracies. The fight is no longer about the issues, as it is about the history of the fight. The longer a war lasts, the longer it's will to end!

Don't get me wrong though, I can understand the dislike and spite towards modern religion. Examine the history of abuse by the Catholic Church. Ordained men shuffled from parish to parish with the crevice of pain upon their hands. The impropriety left as margins of insult for the little boys and girls to overcome. As if apologies or reprimands can cure the silent atrocities betrothed upon them by saintly leadership. The whole situation is sad.

Then you have the big "let's get this money" mega churches. The G5, 100 acre estates, fancy jewelry, and designer suits (Tom Ford). They're on T.V.. every morning requesting a love offering. Love offering? My cable bill and insurance are past due. Pastor got all he could ever need (balling out of control). Pastors' wife comes to church slaying every Sunday.

One thing I can say about churches back in the day– they helped! I can remember Reverend Williams at St. Paul's Baptist church, giving my mother money for the electric bill. I also remember him going to court for my father when he was in trouble. That's what the church use to represent. The church was only as strong as its most fragile member.

Now, the game is all messed up.

I can see why people are critical of churches. They have the right when so much is wrong! Loving God is still a choice. (props to T.D. Jakes)

The obvious choice for me is faith. It gives me balance in a world worn of compassion. Delirium is at the forefront of most murders and hate crimes. People are not born to hurt people. A great quote I once heard states - "hurt people hurt people". So if we are to stand at the gate of hope without a grasp of faith to guide us, than our GPS has no chance.

We should be very scared of a world, where religion is only captured, in its most scandalous tones. Which implodes the motives of those who say "to hell with it!" All they see are reasons why not to embrace faith. We have the responsibility, whether Jewish, Christian, Jehovah's Witness, Muslim, or Catholic, to improve the cautions of perspective believers. We cannot close the doors to those who are misinformed, trepid, or skeptical of authentic places of faith.

If we don't regain a lot of the ground loss to hate, the chance of holy unification will be difficult. It will not be easy, because so much damage has been done. The question of all questions will come up and you must be ready to answer it. - You know the question........ "If God loves us, than why does he allow bad things to happen to us? "Are you ready to answer????

You have to be, 'cause the question may never come again. My answer: "God is not at our disposal to give us perfect lives. All eras of the bible encountered murder, famine, adultery, disease, and pain. God is there to provide hope in times of turmoil. God is there to shepherd us through life and provide an option. God does not bestow evil - evil begets evil. God loves you!"

That's my answer to that most common of questions, regarding Gods' purpose in our lives. I often look at the news and wonder - can we make it back? It seems so far gone. But faith gives us the belief that God can do anything! Evidence of things hoped for.

I kind of miss those early mornings.... Smelling mama's Mary Kay perfume fumigate our apartment. Watching her dart from the kitchen, to the bathroom, and back to the kitchen. Lionel Ritchie's "Jesus is love" bellowing from the speakers. Some good mornings. Sleep crust welled up in the corners of my eyes.

Breathe vaporing the scent of last nights' Doritos and super sweet kool-aid. Riding shot gun in mama's green Nova (old reliable). Navigating the shy Sunday streets of D.C. No gunshots, crackheads looking or prostitutes waving. Sunday serenity.

The parking lot of St. Paul full with churchgoers. Butchie waiting out front for me - his bush picked out neatly. Ms. Maxwell with the polyester navy blue pant suit starched to the nines. A subtle hint of today's treats sprinkled across her face for only I to notice. I'll get out of the green Nova smiling bright.

In a few minutes, the choir is gonna sing "Lift Him Up" so good, that the whole church will go bananas! Then Revvin Williams (Black churches say revvin) gonna preach until that white stuff crowds the corner of his mouth. (What is that white stuff anyway?)

It was so simple then..... Even the cheap church fans meant something, when people waved them. Oh, and that big gulp from 7 eleven - bangin!

All in the name of God. —Or Allah if you prefer. As I reminisce in such opulent hues, God must be laughing.

It is never too late for faith. As Christians, we believe that if you confess that Jesus Christ is your Lord and Savior, and that He died on the cross for your sins, than you will be saved. Saved meaning, when you die, your soul will be passed on to heaven to live forever!

As I stated earlier, faith is a choice. I only ask that if you're void of faith - give it a chance! It really does matter. Life has a different meaning with faith. Faith will keep you in times of trouble. Faith gives you hope. Trust me on this, go to God. He will be there when nobody else is.

quote me....

"People see God every day; they just don't recognize him."

Pearl Bailey NY Times 11/26/1967

3a.m. can't sleep

Please excuse me for extending this chapter. After much thought, I must add more to this chapter. I believe I was way too passive in this chapter. Although this is the short book, no chapter should defy that logic more defiantly than this one. God has been too good to me! He saved my life. I want you to hear my testimony. I will give you the short version. All true and verifiable. God deserves the best in this book - He is truth!

It's like being so true to yourself that even your enemy subscribe to your story. That's what God means to me. So my testimony is a tribute to His power. No word structure, no fear, no regret. God is calling me higher like Shekinah Glory. The bible says "the strong should bare the infirmity."

Mom is the middle girl of 8 sisters and 7 brothers. John, Justin, James, Leonard and now most recently, Aunt Shirley have all passed on. Ruth tried her best with me. Even at birth I was difficult!

I was born on a Sunday morning in Cheverly Md. First few years with ma Ruth was rocky. Slept in the car a few times. Local motels and rooming houses.

All because she loved my dad that much. Granddaddy was not a fan of my dad. "Who was my dad? He was this ultra - slick guy from Baltimore with the fancy clothes and swank sophistication. "Hollywood". Well, that was dads' nickname.

After 24 hours of labor and a C-section, my mother had me. That's love! Mama, I feel compelled to say sorry. I've apologized many times in the past, but tonight's apology is my most sincere.

Mom works legit while Dad works the streets of D.C. (14th street NW). I was there on the front lines like an Afghan. The pimps, stick up boys, and hustlers. The silks and cashmeres. Honor. Street school 101. None of my elementary school classmates (them squares) could have imagined. 'My teachers were fly! My social studies class was hands on. Real geography..

If 14th St. neglected a lesson, the summer evenings on grandma's stoop in Baltimore would fill in. My uncle Poop was like an emperor to me - magic!

The rats, gunfire, and littered syringes could in no way break my attention. I was focused! Poop: jewelry, Benz, respect, and influence. The game had me gone!

I didn't know how gone I was until I woke up in Vegas August 1994. My son still in diapers, suite at Harrods'. It's $45,000 under the bed and I can't stop gambling. The dice got me trapped! My sons mother sleeps the night away - no worries for her.

I crapped out - money gone! At least I got to meet Whitney. She was performing across the street at the MGM Grand. For 90 fleeting seconds, I felt the true essence of a star. RIP.

How I blew 45k in a couple nights is still puzzling? It was mama's idea to move us to MPLS anyway. Chasing behind my dad who was approved to attend the Hazelden drug treatment in Minnesota. All I kept hearing was 'world renowned treatment center'. Before I knew it, we were leaving Maryland and heading to Princes' town (Purple Rain). A huge reason I was in Vega$ in the first place.

Long story short...... my dad became friends with Alexander O'Neal at Hazelden. Dad convinced Alex to take me to a show whenever in D.C. Well actually, Alex was the show!

Alex was always on BET. He was even on my radio most nights. Now he was out front of our apartment, and mama is dressed to the nines. Of course, I played it cool. I had been around stars all my life - who was this country boy taking mama and I to Constitution Hall? The limo looked like a spaceship!

The whole night, I was backstage feeling like royalty. I told the Force MD's Alex was my uncle. Just another day in the life of a 7th grader. I went to school the next day and told nobody. Who would believe me anyway? The paparazzi, the lights, mama and I riding the limo down Rhode Island Avenue pass our old apartment (3217). It felt like life.. It felt like the game. And I enjoyed every moment of it!

That night changed my life. It was that night with Alex that had me in Vegas. The allure of lights. The money, no different than other money blown. I had been in Vegas the year before with Eric and Al for my 18th birthday. Convertible stretch limo with the Gucci loafers on. Too much exposure by age 19. But the effects of squandering that 45k was deep!

I never told my sons mother. All we had leaving Vegas was $3,000 cash and a white Jeep Cherokee. I bought it off the lot with the emergency money I had stashed in my sons diapers. It was a long, quiet ride to Oklahoma City where my sons' mothers' family resided. A long, painful ride........

It was always about the next hotel, limo, city, or state. By age 21, I had hit 35 states and stayed long enough to live in 5 of them. My life from 14 to 24 is a blur! No two days were the same. One thing that was the same; my commitment to my kids. Whether in Minneapolis, Oklahoma, North Carolina, Maryland or wherever, I needed my kids. My children gave me balance.

But the streets were just in me.... I could bust a kilo of coke down and sell it hand to hand. Or easily manufacture stolen credit cards and shop for days. When I got tired of that, I would fence stolen laptop computers 10 at a time. One thing for sure - I was gonna get some money.

I don't have that story of having $200,000 hidden under my mothers' mattress. If I saved $ 30,000, I would spend $30,000. All I know is money was never a factor! I would literally go through $5,000 after $5,000 a week for years on lifestyle. Mama once asked me to put an estimate on those 10 years money wise. I can't. It was too much and credit card money can't be counted.

So that's the monster that was created from those days uptown with dad. That's what D.C. days and Baltimore nights started. I was lost! Men were killed in front of me.

I myself even accused of murder once. Detective Pete Jackson in Minneapolis tried to make me admit to killing someone I didn't. The whole 90's "bright light" intimidation interrogation story. Back when they use to smack you to start the conversation. Real shit!

Those 10 years almost destroyed my life! It was always bail money needed, and trying to remember aliases. I had accustomed 6 official aliases. I always wondered, "why did God spare me?"

Then one night while on my way to a Lakers game, I saw the end coming. God came to me clear as day and said I was gonna get in a lot of trouble. He said if I believed in him, he would get me through it. The voice was so real.

As clear as the night in 1998 when the devil propositioned me as I sat in my car. In the car with me: 20 laptops in the trunk and $100,000 in stolen jewelry on my lap. The devil then spoke to me.....

His words exactly....Turn left and I will give you the world. This is the truth! The devil tempted me. YES - the devil! I didn't think twice, I told the devil I was going right. God was more important than all the devil promised me.

But this vision of God was way more vivid. As I chilled in my hotel room preparing to see Shaq and Kobe play K.G., I had a decision to make. I told God I would trust him.

I'm telling you, God is real!

Right after the Lakers and Timberwolves game, my mother called on cue. She said the F.B.I. was in Oklahoma City looking for me. Over the next 2 months my life unraveled in warp speed! The house on Tremont was raided; cars, jewelry, and money squandered. Warrants in multiple states for a variety of offenses - and stress. God told me it was coming!

On the day that I got arrested, I felt it. I had this weird lump it my throat. Never felt anything like it before. As I pulled out to take my wife to work (friends at the time) D.C. police cruiser was waiting for me. After a short chase in my truck and then on foot, I was arrested. I was taken to D.C. headquarters and questioned thoroughly. I never said anything.

Now, over 17 years later, God has been so merciful to me! I had to just trust him through it all. It was not easy. A lot of people died and life has moved on. But I still felt life. Still had my kids. I've never really spoken about all of this. I've never wanted to appear as one to glorify that life. Many people who know me have no idea.

I was also too ashamed of mistakes I've made. I had to ask God humbly for forgiveness. I asked for years! He gave me comfort and said he still loved me. GOD STILL LOVES ME! I can say that boldly.

He loved me from that Sunday morning I was born. He's loved me throughout my mistakes. In spite of the hardness of incarceration, the ignorance of my childhood perceptions, and everything else - he loves me!

He gave me a loving and grounded wife. My best friend and better half. We both acknowledge God daily, as he protects our blended family. I love you so much Sweets, and owe much of many change to you. Always *71-75*!

My Father faced Trials and Tribulations in the past, and made it through them by the graces of God. My mom and dad gave marriage an honest try. She was loyal to pack up and move to Minnesota for her husband. I was just a 14 year old rolling with his mother. This woman ALWAYS prayed for me. I could call her at 4 in the morning in Chicago, and she would get up and pray. Mama is a devoted follower of Jesus.

My kids are good people and none of them are living that type of life. One daughter happily married and the other in college. Two sons working and trying to figure it out. God has blessed me with giving them good, simple lives. The burden was mine to carry. As for me....... I'm happily married and trying to make an impact in life. My wife and I feel that this book is needed. Especially when so many people are lost. When I start slipping, my wife would say "alright homie tighten up." Her story a book in itself. The story of a woman who has been protected by God through many challenges.

I really give God thanks for even the idea of this book. For being alive! I could have died all those nights running the streets: hustling, clubs, shootouts, hate, and envy. I also could have life in prison. So God is beyond good!

I feel a lot better that I didn't leave this out the book. Maybe it will give you more perspective on who's writing to you. It's never been easy for me to talk about myself. I've always been a good listener. I hope you still accept me, my baggage, and life's flaws. I know if you don't - at least God will.

3

Oreo....Cracker....Nigga.

Much debate has been made about the Confederate flag. Its history, symbolism, and place in American culture. Many supporters point to their heritage as the catalyst of that support. Many opponents refer to the painful history left by the civil war. The Confederate soldiers fought to keep slavery - that's a fact! So here's what I don't understand...... If you knew that something triggered so much pain and horrific memories, would you still stand by it? Even if it offended millions of Americans? I would say that's very selfish!

I just went old school racist on ya'll. Oreo, cracker, nigga..... I'm in my 40's, and those are the racial epithets I can remember being slung around in my childhood. The Oreo was the Bryant Gumble and Clarence Thomas types. Cracker symbolized White people. And we all know who the nigga was for. Nigga is a lot softer than NIGGER. It matters too that *-i-g-g-e-r* is more harsh than *i-g-g-a*. Less painful.

Where am I going with this? Stop playing with your square ass! You know where I'm going. I'm going right at you coward, hatin, bigoted, fake, spiteful, covert and situational racists! Yeah I said it! Somebody has to! If I'm gonna win that most coveted Pulitzer (that I intend on donating) I guess I need to nail this chapter. Wish me luck!

The responsibility of getting an issue right that so many people got wrong, is pressure. Everybody has tried to talk about it, but no one has quite got it right. Dr. Cornell West, Angela Davis, Malcom X, Martin Luther King Jr., David Duke, Condoleeza Rice, Bush Sr., Bush Jr., Oprah, Spike Lee, Lebron, Tiger Woods, and Obama have all addressed it. Some did it in taste, and some with haste, but at least they tried.

The great Maya Angelou, Kanye, Madonna, Beyonc'e, Ryan Gossling, Rodney King, John Lennon, Trayvons' parents and Mike Browns' too..... Hillary, the Black Lives Matter movement, April Duvernay, Shonda Rhimes, and Rosa Parks. Want more??

Well, let's go Ferguson, Donald Trump, Bobby Deniro, Denzel Washington, John Stewart, Johnny Cash, Abraham Lincoln, J.F.K, Mike Wallace, Soledad, CNN, ESPN, Fox, Cracker Barrel, and even New York City cab drivers. Had enough yet? I'll go one more round for good measure.

Baltimore police, D.C. police, Houston police, Dallas police, Los Angeles police, NAACP, Rachel Dolezal, Mel Gibson, the goofy guy from Seinfeld, The Oscars, Globes, Emmy's, Grammys, Jay Leno, Common, John Legend, The Kardashians, Frank Sinatra, and more. Alright I'm tired now.

This list is not even a percent of the people, businesses, or dignitaries that have spoken on race one time or another. Many have tried and some were effective. Some did it by choice (CNN). Some by force (Baltimore police). Some out of anger (Mel Gibson).

My fault Mel, really loved *Passion of the Christ*, but you were out of order!

The whole getting a bunch of black guys to rape your girlfriend comment - dead wrong!

I thought you and Danny Glover were tight. Let me get back on message before I really go at Mel.

The truth is, many have spoken on it, but nobody has nailed it! I thought Obama did well with what he had to work with. I was also captivated by CNN'S transparency in a set of documentaries they did on Race in

America. Soledad really nailed those pieces. I'm confused as to why she's on PBS now. She should own CNN in my opinion.

But my go to person on race relations oddly enough, is Whoopi Goldberg. Whoopi's moderator seat on *The View* has presented her many opportunities to hide behind political correctness and sponsorship. But Whoopi has her mojo working! What I really like about Whoopi is her honesty. She states facts about race that clearly define the perspectives of the voiceless.

I also know from Whoopi's past, that she's no pro black extremist. She ran with Billy Crystal, Robin Williams, and was even cool with Elizabeth Taylor. Plus she's dated a lot of white men - Ted Danson the most soulful. My hat goes off to Whoopi.

For those who spoke on race for fame or publicity - shame on you! I cherish Maya Angelou for writing one of our Nation's most healing poems. She read it at President Clinton's inauguration. Google it and hear the eloquence and soaring crescendo in which this great woman spoke. Unafraid on the biggest stage. Priceless!

Yet in still, with all the grumbling, mumbling, tumbling, and stumbling, race has garnered, no one has been able to reach both sides equally.

The voice of a unifying race address has yet to be accomplished. Maybe such a feat is not possible inside of the human framework. To possess the love, compassion, honesty, openness, and trepidation in one individual thesis on race, would be almost impossible.

Truth be told. Each and every person of a certain age has had evil race manifestations gnawing at them. So to put aside pride, anger, embarrassment, mistrust, and many other internal ailments and speak of clairvoyant thought is tough! But that does not mean it's unachievable.

In the months leading up to this past election, Donald Trump spearheaded a hate catalogue that spurred even the most silent of racists. Hate crimes are up against Jewish, African American, LGBT, Muslims, and Hispanics. Trump will quickly say, "oh, I love everybody" while side-stepping the fact that his hateful undertones play a factor on society. To stand in front of a camera and spew insults at a race or religion is inciting actions. That makes Kenny in West Virginia, or Paul in Omaha, think that it's okay. "Trump hates - so we can hate!"

For us to pretend that race related comments or innuendos has no bearing on day to day life, is not just callous, but also naive. Words do hurt, and they have the ability to break down. They also can build you up!

The sensitivity behind race is always going to be there. It's like the groundhog peeking its head out to see if it sees its shadow.

Race in many ways is that groundhog, unsure of what to expect. The thing I don't agree with, is when people say "why is everybody so sensitive about race?" Why? If there is a cultural emotive that should bring sensitivity- it should be race!

The pain and sorrow is like a long winding road that has no stop signs or exits.

It should be handled with the utmost care and concern. For the history of its origins is deeply rooted inside of Americas' fabric. As kin to America is apple pie, so too is racism. Tolerance is necessary, for true healing to ever exist. NEVER question why people are so race sensitive.

We must realize that many of our Nations' shameful moments of race, have been played out for the world to see. The riots and marches of the 60's are on reel. The black bodies hanging from trees in Mississippi. The dogs biting and water hoses spraying. Black billy clubs banging against Black heads. The opposition? People who only wanted human rights.

We even watched the Rodney King beating play out before our eyes. Images still piercing the soul to many of us. Speed up to the issues happening right now in the 2017: Our trusted police are accruing dead bodies, for what they say was a sudden move. Or a cell phone resembled a gun.

Over the past 5 years, situation after situation has been captured by cell phones for the world to see. A man shot in the back as he ran away in

South Carolina; a man gunned down in the middle of the street after being accused of stealing cigars at a convenience store in Ferguson Missouri; one more gunned down in his car with his girlfriend and her daughter, as he reaches in his pocket for his carriers permit in St. Paul, Minnesota. Let's not specify that these men were black - these men were human beings!

Right now I pray that anybody who is reading this, will open their hearts and hear my words with love. I pray that you will not get defensive or angry towards my words. I pray that you accept my view of racism as true and unjudging. I love you for being human. I pray that you love me for the same reason. Human.

The pain of slavery has never fully been recovered from for whites or blacks. Here are the facts: Africans were beaten, kidnapped, shackled, and thrown on ships. They were fed slop, dehumanized, and tortured. For those who wanted to buck the system; they were killed and thrown overboard.

Take a second if you will and make that personal. Whether you are White, Black, Asian, Hispanic, Italian, French, you name it - make this personal!

You are taken across the Atlantic Ocean on a ship, shackled like a dog, leaving behind all you've ever known. Afraid and unsure of tomorrow's probability.

The ship takes months to arrive.....Once arriving on America shores (for those who made it), you are moved like herd to the auction block. You then find out they're SELLING HUMANS. Let me say that one more time..... THEY ARE SELLING HUMANS! It just got real.

Now, your only fault is being physically strong. For here (on the block, muscles are rewarded. These same muscles that once helped you hunt for food in the jungles of Africa, are now your achilles heel. Imagine that, my strength becoming my weakness.

You are quickly auctioned off to a white man you've never met before. He's smiling the whole time and patting you on the back. A small part of you begins to believe that this smiling white man, is gonna save you from this nightmare! Your mind is racing in concern for your Queen and kids left back home.

But reality has you on this wagon in Virginia.

Snap back to reality, it's getting real! The same man who was smiling moments ago, is now looking with the evil eyes of 10 scorned spouses. Words are being said to you that make no sense. The only language you've ever known lives nowhere near this new dialect invading your ears. But it's all about survival..... shackled to this wagon you are still surviving.

You arrive on an open piece of land with a lot of people tending to it. People who look like you - but who are they?

Aggressive men come to grab you off the wagon. They strip you naked and yell things at you. They laugh.... spit on you - beat you - and demoralize you. Why are they so excited? You have no words to say. Your words are no good here. So you do all that you know- SURVIVE.

You work most days into the evening. You eat out of the pig pin with the hogs. Brutally beaten for not agreeing to a name that's not yours. Yet you survive...and survive. After moons and suns for years you realize..... This is my life.

You are forced to breed with a woman you've never known. Together you bare a son. The same men who beat you, take your queens body for their own pleasure. Hurt and anger swell your spirit. Yet and still - you survive.

Now your son is on the front lines. He's strong like you and knows the secret word...... Survive. His name is John. Late into Johns' life one day, he overhear field slaves muttering something about being free. He pretends not to hear out of fear.

He's the top hand in the masters' house, and how would this freedom thing affect that? So he does all that he knows....He survives.

He stays by his masters' side, even after his children and grandchildren leave in hopes of finding this freedom word. He dies alone one August evening on his master's porch, with a glass of ice tea, sweating from the Virginia heat. He dies a free slave. Irony...

The point of this story, was not to rehash the old bloody wounds of slavery. It was only to simplify the journey of what has become cliché. That pain was real, and it passed from generation to generation. Try asking Black people why they don't like to swim. Many will draw a blank. For my money - it's due to those ships!

Psychological damage can kill the will in generations. These facts give African Americans the right to be mad. The same way the Native Americans and Jews can be angry. The holocaust happened! Don't take that away from a race who endured ugly remnants of history. To say I'm not crying as I type this, would be a lie. It's been over 400 years and it still stirs emotion.

Let's speed up now to other things that factor into racism in America. Please do not feel pro or anti, in any respect to my description of history. Nobody reading this is right or wrong for sins committed 400 years ago. You are only wrong if you still hold dear to the scripts that were enacted by the characters then. I say characters because, they were but figments of what they thought history demanded them to be. Americans knew nothing about Africans. America really had no reference of itself. When something is unprecedented, where is understanding retained from?

So America was only thinking about America; building America was Americas only priority. Those are the facts.....

Now, here's my issue.... If that was 400 years ago; then why in the 1960's were "Americans" fighting to ride on the front of a bus? These Black Americans basic rights of drinking water from a fountain, or using a public bathroom should've long been settled. Colored only signs in the 60's? It seems like the dew of slavery extended too far. Next year will mark 50 years since the assassination of Martin Luther King Jr. Just 50 years ago. That's only a few generations since Kings' assassination. So yes, we have come a long way with pop culture, Barack Obama, and even race acceptance; but we are talking 400+ years. Let me bring this into even clearer focus....

More work needs to be done. Just saying "get over it" is very unfair. What we are dealing with now, is the hearts of people - nothing more nothing less! The barriers have been broken. There are no excuses that any dream of human achievement is possible!

This is directed squarely at African Americans. We cracked the code! Trap soul, ex hustler writing books. We have judges, lawyers, doctors, politicians, teachers, scholars, and professors, Obama. I'd rather say that than Lebron, Beyonc'e, or Chance the rapper. The scope is broader. The ability to rise is available to all now.

I will say that some in impoverished situations, are in more debilitating realities than others. That is just a cold hard fact. A lot of what you become, coincides with what you are exposed to. Good home, good school, good neighborhood = good life. At least your odds are better.

The reality of some peoples' lives, may be realities you will never face. I'm on a roll now.......

I want to share with you something I've never told anyone. I was the victim of racism on many occasions in my life. Many of those situations I have been too angry to speak on. But I will tell you one that happened when I was 17 years old. The culprit? A Minneapolis police officer.

After being stopped by a police officer for really nothing, he approached my drivers' side window. Then for some reason, he demanded I get out of the car. He didn't ask, my name, do you have a license nothing! I was placed in the back of his cruiser with the windows rolled up. He adjusted his rear view mirror and stared at me for what seemed to be hours.

"You Black nigger piece of shit! I will fucking kill you and nobody would care!" Say something so I can beat your ass....Say something nigger! I was frozen and confused. The stitches of my shorts melting into his police cruisers seat.

I was a street dude by nature at that time, but I was still terrified.

I will never forget it for as long as I live, the anger he had towards me was startling. What did I do to him? Why was he so angry? I wonder, if I were to see him again today, 25 years later, would he feel the same way?

Today is the first time I've told anybody. Of course my wife and mother would say, "why didn't you tell me?" A part of me just wanted to forget. Then a part of me was embarrassed for being so scared. A man and his manhood can be very complicated.......

I am sure that many African Americans have stories just like mine.

Stories lying dormant inside the attics of their memories. That one night riding home from work. That early morning walk to the corner store. Too many....

It calls me to question why does racism still exist? How can someone hate someone they know nothing about? It's just wrong! It's also wrong for us as African Americans, to say all White people are racist. That's not true at all. If you relook at some of those 60's reels of the civil rights movement, you will see White Americans fighting and going to jail with Black Americans. I wonder if those images have done more harm than good? The paranoia can be a lot to process.

Which brings me to the most symbolic landscape of race in our Nations' history; the Civil War. The Civil War was without question the most pivotal moment in Americas' race history. It gave people the right to pick a side. But not only pick a side, you could fight and die for your sides beliefs.

Many of us overlook the enormity of that red/blue north/south dueling. To say it was the war on slavery, would be correct in tone and accuracy. To say it constructed a line throughout America is even more true. Americans fighting Americans to enslave Americans. The declared America that is. The first real oxymoron.

So each side has accountability to accept. Racism against any race in 2017 is no longer acceptable. It must stop! Even in lieu of the rash of police

Life Is So . . . You Know | 35

shootings over the past few years. That's been there for decades, but the ability for us as Americans to video it has not been. Here's a serious question to you... Are the police shootings about race, power, or lack of training?

In most urban communities race is the reality. If I'm a White police officer in South Philly, 80% of the people I encounter will be African American. Is that a race issue, or is that a demographic reality?

The reality also says that these inner cities are more violent and perplexing to police, than say Bethesda Maryland. So can we definitively say that each and every officer is racist? Or are they White officers, working in predominantly high violence Black neighborhoods, where violence just happens? Think about that a second...

My second question was the power factor. Are these police officers so brazen in their ability to get away with something, that they will not hesitate to do it? Is the blue wall of security so protected, that officers neglect sound judgement in anticipation of being protected for brazen actions?

If I know my station commander has my back because he's my poker buddy, maybe I'm at liberty to react to a situation recklessly, rather than follow protocol. My last question is whether there is lack of training. Are these officers being trained adequately enough to patrol these neighborhoods? Do they know the schematics of these neighborhoods? The plight? The triggers? Do they know that hot summer nights are more hostile than spring mornings? Can they read body language as to who really wants a problem, as to someone who may have mental health problems? Are they in tune with the hood, or just patrolling the hood?

There is a way to de-escalate many situations in the inner cities. Most men and women do not want to die.

Sometimes it's the frustrations and strain of the conditions that predicate the action. How can police receive better training? Maybe men and women who know the streets, could offer lectures and real insight into its genetics.

I ask these questions because the murders have been heart wrenching. The cell phone footage has been unbelievable to watch. I can see myself inside of those split second life changing events. I hustled in the hood; shot basketball in the hood; I feel the hood! So it was personal to me when the bodies were popping up all over the country.

I also had to check myself from assuming it was by racist officers. Let me admit, I was the first one to say "these White police keep killin us!" I was hot! Until I had to stop and think...... My thinking brought me to these three questions....1. Are they racist? 2. Is it the power? 3. Is it lack of training?

I am asking you to examine these three questions also. Because whichever the three it is, it has to be corralled. We cannot let men, women, or children, under any circumstance, fall at the hands of the very people who are sworn to protect them. We must speak out!

I've laid out a comprehensive framework of our Nations race history. I could write for days on the gravity of racism, its history and pit falls. I chose to delve into the topics that have challenged us as a nation. I chose not to touch the O.J. Simpson fiasco, for the media will be dissecting that for years to come!

So what do you think? Can we pull ourselves up and ascend to a higher level as a nation? Is race really that serious anymore, or are we afraid to let it go?

Are we doing a good enough job? Are you doing your part? Let's join together in stamping out the ignorance of racism, its stereotypes, and labeling.

It's been 400 years my dear American. That's four centuries, countless generations, and many stories. The world is only getting more diverse. No matter how many walls Trump attempts to build, the inner workings of America builds diversity.

This open missive to you about race was not about judging. This was not me saying bad-bad White people. This was about understanding the dynamics of race and its traditions. This is about unity....

The chapter heading says Oreo, Cracker, Nigga. We are neither. We are beautifully crafted people with smiles, styles, ideals, and dreams. You must sit down with your friends and family and discuss what's next. What generation will stop this genocide of grotesque ignorance?

Who will say 400 years has been enough? We don't need another book or movie - we need action! Enough with the talking and lectures. We've had 400 years of those. Each person now has to stand up and say no!

Say "NO" if you were taught racism from your father or mother. Say "NO" when one of your friends slide in a Mexican joke. Have the guts to go against hate!

To all those who came before me on the race issue, I say thank you. I would be remised if I forgot Michael Eric Dyson. He has always had profound and introspective ways of looking at race. But let me say this again, Whoopi is my girl on race discussions. Watch The View, when you have time, they always confront race and issues of importance.

I want to close with I love you. If you are a racist, I love you. You can change the way you think. To truly know an individual, is to truly know the person! Say "NO" to racism and its undertones. Say "NO" to its ugly history. The ignorance. The traits. This is for all nationalities and races. This book is the tool to unite! Stand with me - say NO! Racism must end!

quote me......

"We all grow up with the weight of history on us. Our ancestors dwell in the attics of our brains as they do in the spiraling chains of knowledge hidden in every cell of our bodies."

Shirley Abbott

A moment of your time.

On March 6<th> 2017, a formal apology from the Roger B. Taney family to the Dred Scott family, was extended on the grounds of the Maryland State House. Robert B. Taney, who was U.S. Chief justice at the time of the March 6<th> 1857 Dred Scott decision, still has a statue on the Maryland State House grounds.

In the Dred Scott decision, Chief Justice Taney ruled that Congress could not regulate slavery and that Blacks could not be considered U.S. Citizens. Dred Scott, a slave from Missouri had filed motion for his freedom and other issues of urgency to him.

Charles Taney III, a descendant of Justice Taney and Lynne Jackson of St. Louis, great-great granddaughter of Dred Scott, hugged at the very spot of Justice Raneys' statue. Mr. Taney stated "apologizing to the Scotts for the Dred Scott decision is like bringing a Band-Aid to an amputation." He also stated that," it's right and necessary to apologize, but what's important now is what actions we can all take to bring about racial reconciliation."

The apology was spurred on by Charles Taney III's daughter Kate Taney-Billingsley, who grew up hearing relatives debate whether the family should apologize to the Scott Family. She asked herself, "what do you do with that kind of generational guilt?" Kate decided to write a play titled, A Man of His Time. Which, premiered at The Actors Studio in New York last year. - Baltimore Sun Newspaper

So maybe it is never too late. -160 years.

4

Love / Hate

Ashley Graham is a model. People who are familiar with Ashley, will concur on her beauty. Yet, she's labeled as a plus sized model. What is plus size? Each size is a size. At what size does it become plus? Why the distinct ion? If you really think about it, it's extremely vain and foolish! Why are we agreeing to label a woman a "plus sized model?" I must be naive to think that such a statement is emotionally damaging too many. To be categorized by size must stop!

The power of love is intoxicating. It has the ability to strengthen, and even the bravery to heal. Love is the strongest emotion or feeling known to mankind.

Love is always there, twisting and turning through problems. Love just is......

When a baby is born, what's the first thing the doctor does? He lifts the baby for inspection, and then passes the baby to the mother. The newborn lays there upon the bosom of the mother. In that most tender of moments, the newborn rests. The mother softly consoles the newborn. That's love!

I have always been a loving person.

That does not mean I haven't done things that were not reflective of love. I think we all have had our moments. But love has always had a stronger pull on my life.

I can remember as a child, always wanting to help people. I wanted to help my mother, aunts, grandmother, lady next door - whoever! It would make me feel good to make someone else feel good. Paying the love forward....

That part of my personality comes from my mother. My mother has always been a loving person. Her heart is pure gold! To have compassion without instigation is a gift of love. Love without conditions.

I could put together a florilegium of writings that would tackle a plethora of love dynamics. Love is no joke! I am helplessly in love with my wife. We have been on a 20 year love affair full of ups and some downs. There were times where we both probably doubted it would last. It has! We can firmly attribute communication and friendship to our longevity.

The world is full of love and hate these days. People almost love to hate.

A lot of the fuel has been triggered by social media, and society's insatiable craving for scandal. It has become a standard practice for people to sit behind laptops and smart phones, typing away on other peoples' lives. We are all critics now!

We were all given the choice to like or dislike. - We ran with it! The critique demand on our psyche was subtle. We were constantly asked to rate services: food, clothing, furniture, communities, and just about everything else. Like me on Facebook.

Say hello to Angie's List. A welcomed help if used properly. Let the wrong person on Angie's List, and there goes your reputation.

Let me say this respectfully... Everybody is not capable of giving critique. Some people just have a skewered way of looking at things. Words are misunderstood, intentions are misread. That's why you had Siskel and Ebert or Derrick and Annie!

Before we knew it, our expertise in critique was spilling over into who was dressed best - fashion police (the late Joan Rivers). Then the responsibility of choosing who's most beautiful. Well, People magazine does that once a year. That in turn brought internet bullying and social media trolls looking for a victim. Now the line between love and hate is thin as ever!

Mama and I were tight during my childhood. I was her son, part time counselor, confidante, and more. Maybe those roles were more than my adolescent mind was prepared to handle, but I didn't know any better. Things were tough, and it was my duty to stand by my mother.

Today's love is fleeting. Marriages have a 50% chance of lasting.

The effort is no longer there. My grandparents were married 50+ years. They did it while raising fifteen children. I was fortunate to spend quality time with them as a child (Often times I was suspended from school).

I remember watching them have these explosive arguments about menial things. I hat up in your face "what's up" arguing. Their voices were loud and tempers would flare, but the love was never relinquished. It was amazing to me. After a solid hour of screaming at each other, my grandmother would break off script and say "what do you want for dinner?" Then my grandfather would respond as if nothing happened, "pepper steak and rice." No hard feelings.

As we sat down at the table to eat dinner, no signs of animosity. I grew up naively expecting that same type of love. Any woman who wanted me, better know how to argue, and fix me scrambled eggs with a smile. Do you think it worked? - Hell no!

Females in the 90's/2000's were not going for that. Their response, "Fix you something to eat? Dude are you crazy!" So maybe I was stupid to expect that 50's type of love in the hard 90's. Love is not what it used to be.

Maybe it's the enormous amount of hate that's drowning out the love. People hate short people, tall people, thin people, fat people, rich people, and poor people. They even hate Jewish people, White people, Black people, Christians, Muslims, Catholics, and more! Women hate on other women, and men hate on other men. Hate has become the new normal in our society. Here's the problem.....The problem is, a lot of us are unhappy.

People are working unfulfilling jobs, enduring bad marriages, and separating from their families. Many are out here going through hell. Trying to find happy!

I truly believe that if unhappiness is left unchecked, it can inadvertently turn to hate! That's why you find yourself lashing out during road rage situations. "You dumb bastard, why you cut me off?" (sound familiar)? The deception of anger masked as rage.

I have never hated a person. Is that hard to believe? My word to you - I haven't. I have been disappointed. I've always heard "hate is such a strong word." I always thought love was a strong word.

Women will often say, "I hate that b###h!"" Most people who spew such venom, were hurt by love. That woman probably stole her man. How can a once great love turn so sour and bitter?

All of us know a mother, sister, friend, etc., who's been hurt. A man whom she loved, had no regards for her family. But she kept giving him chance after chance. That's usually when her best girlfriend says, "he must have some good sex girl!" Love has a way of blinding the instincts.

A woman's hate for a man who hurt her can run deep! No worse enemy than a woman scorned. Heartbreak is rarely handled in good taste. Why hurt a good woman? They were not born to be relationship prey. Our women have endured enough heartache. My mother included, but she never turned bitter. Or was that her poker face on display? All I know is my dad left her holding loves bag. She still displayed grace and class.

Here's a long story small book short.....

Dad completes Hazelden treatment and moves in with his sponsor. Sponsor being a middle aged Wisconsin woman with a warm demeanor and truck driver husband. A truck driving husband that was gone for weeks on end. Insert my Baltimore raised, D.C. bred father, armed with charm and loads of charisma. The mid-western sponsor never seen him coming. Early morning cups of coffee and late night talks. No more intrigue is needed for this one - the obvious happened. They have now been together for over 25 years. Let's go back early 90's if you will....

My dad's playing Latin lover living comfy; meanwhile, my mother and I are living cramped in some lady's basement. I'm 13 trying to understand why are we here? Mama not feeling it. Dad, in Wisconsin eating that good cheese, while we scratch and claw. Kind of funny looking back at it now.

My mothers' only mistake??? - loving a man. She loves him so much that she packs all our stuff, and puts it on a U-Haul truck. Now we're here, and dad rarely comes to visit us in Minneapolis. Why won't he play house with us?

You see, it's not that he convinced her to move us halfway across country. That's the cost of commitment. It wasn't even the violation of sponsor - patient etiquette. Neither was it the woman being White. It was the fact that he never came out and kept it real, really hurt mama. The lies kept coming! Mama never complained though. All is fair in love and war. She made a life in Minneapolis. Kept pushing! That doesn't mean she got over it immediately. I think it took her years to recover completely. On that course of recovery, I never heard her hate. She was a woman bamboozled out of her life, and she never hated.

The love/hate line of 2017 is real! Friend today and enemy tomorrow. Steve Harvey meets Donald Trump and he gets death threats. Bartman interferes with a ball at a Cubs game and people want to kill him.

Hate has too many echelons: There's life hate - work hate - religious hate- social media hate - community hate - family hate - body shaming hate - fraternity hate - race hate - political hate - LGBT hate - hate, hate, hate!

Love is desperate to be loved again. We are all too hard and too out of touch! We have lost loves touch. Ya'll gonna hate me for kickin this raw to you. As if I could hide the truth from you. You need the truth!

All of the images and clips of hate has desensitized our world. Our minds are processing it, and neatly tucking it into our subconscious. We move on to the next task. Then we go to work at 8am like nothing's wrong.

On June 17, 2015 Dylan Roof enters a Bible study class at Emanuel AME church in Charleston, South Carolina. The all Black bible study group welcomes Dylan with open arms. Dylan sits quietly and observes. The plan has been etched in his mind for months.

As the group bows their heads in prayer - he shoots them. The nerve of him, to shoot heads bowed. Nine people are murdered...

A week before the shooting, Dylan confided in childhood friend Joey Meek, about his hate for Black people. He tells Joey his plan. Dylan's exact words were, "I hate Black people and I'm going to a church in Charleston to kill them." Joey Meek would tell authorities only after Dylan's actions.

What if Joey had told Dylan NO? What if Joey had just hugged Dylan and told him he loved him? What if the smallest act of kindness was displayed? History might have changed. If you know of someone fixated with hate that could harm others, would you remain silent?

The term "going postal" is in reference to rogue Americans with guns. It's like snapping on life.

The most recent instance was Mr. Steven Stephens. Stephens thought it relieving to murder an old innocent man on Facebook live. Mr. Stephens would eventually murder himself, after days of a Nation - wide manhunt.

Did you see this? Do you remember? How did you respond? Did you keep sipping your caramel macchiato in perfect timing? Are you in the matrix of life? Do you know it?

The hippie movement was epic. Love is all we need backed by good weed and L.S.D. Peace signs stitched on hats and shirts. The movement saw the perils of violence as our biggest threat. The violence of Vietnam. The increased violence on innocent people. The hippies knew of an impending fate on society. We should have listened.

Mother Theresa, Mahatma Gandhi, Martin Luther King Jr., Pope John Paul II, Anne Frank, Kahlil Gibran, Dalai Lama, and so many more have been love agents. They spoke to the earth with compassion, no matter which corner they were on. All voices of love for humanity. I don't hear those voices anymore!

Oprah Winfrey and Ellen DeGeneres are the most giving television personalities I've ever seen. Giving is a form of love. To give without expectance, even more special. Are you a giver or receiver? Do you still love even when you don't receive what you expected?

I always tell my wife that people in society are weird and out of touch! Her response, "why do you say that baby?" I then go into a 20 minute synopsis on the callous hearts in society. The murders, violence, and disregard for life. A "doggy dog world" as Snoop Dog once rapped.

Even our families lack love now. Gone are the Bunkers, Cosby's, Jefferson's, and Partridge's. Now, it's The Real Housewives of: *pick a city*. Family's use to eat together, support each other, and honor that family bond. Now we got cell phones at the dinner table. We are so busy that we speak to each other in passing. Shout out to all the family's that still act like family.

This next issue I must address is risky. It may cause some *black* lash but it has to be said. This book is undone without saying this.....(16)

Black on Black hate! Who's the flyest, who wore it best, = competition! We always try to outdo each other. Twitter and Facebook blazing with hate!

The common phrase in our community is "stop hating." 50 cent said "hate it or love it the under dogs on top." Listen to the music we love so affectionately, and all you hear is hate. Hater this, hater that, hater get off my back!

Black men have been killing Black men for decades. Killing for money, for position, and even for women. Die for a new pair of Jordan's. Die for how you look at somebody. We pose with guns and money for Facebook and Twitter fans to see. I guess that's cool now days.

Black on Black hate in my eyes is the worst hate! White people can be racist to Black people; Religious groups can judge lesbian, bi, gay, and transgender people; skinny people can hate fat people. But none of these people are gunning down the other every day. Black men have been waring since Reagan was in. In some city right now - there's a beef!

People who know, know! I can say it, I lived on those streets. I lost people on those streets. Why are we not outraged? What's going on in Chicago is an American tragedy. The same in D.C., Gary, Indiana, Baltimore, Miami, Philly, Richmond, Virginia, and New Orleans.

Where's Jesse Jackson and Al Sharpton? Where's the Black Lives Matter movement? Where are the actors, rappers, and stars? Where are the politicians and activists? Blood is running down the streets, and we turn a blind eye.

Do you hate me now for kicking this real? Somebody has to say it! It's easy to say it when the cameras are rolling. Say it with a heavy heart and tears streaming down your face. I love the Black Lives Matter movement, and the activists that are involved. I just wonder how long will we kill each other, before each person is willing to die to save another's life.

Men, women and children have been dying for way too long. We show up at a vigil, light a candle, and resume life afterwards. Funerals have become no more than a fashion show and place to catch up. If you know, than you know this is true.

We scream and holler when a White officer harms people of color, but remained silent when people of color hurt each other. Research the numbers and see the stats of Black on Black homicides.

The numbers are crazy! It all comes back to hate. Hate of self, circumstances, and conditions. This is the REAL elephant in the room.

My heart goes out to Eric Gardener, Mike Brown, Trayvon Martin, and all the other innocent men, women, and children killed by law enforcement. But my heart also goes out to Mook, lil' Reggie, Black, and Tony. Their lives matter also.

I want to force my truth on you in this book. It's not my goal for us to be enemies, but better yet comrades. My life has been deftly scarred by mistakes, which leaves me impotent of judgement. I do know of this hate I speak on. - It exists! This almost feels like an extension of chapter 3: Oreo, Cracker, Nigga. For much of this Black on Black hate was siphoned from slavery's womb. The house nigga, versus the field nigga, holding crucial positioning rights for status.

The same positioning battles stand today. We want to dress the best, look the best, talk the best, and appear the best. We salivate over entertainment beefs. Love and hate should not be so close in proximity.

We all need healing. Life presents a maze of adversities and issues that become us! It's not easy, and the mere allusion that it is - is wrong! Our humanity needs to be re-humanized. If I tell you the truth about what's happening, will you take rebuke it? It's only truth!

Religious and social hate corrupts the spirit. The spirit is not attracted to hate by choice. Remember, the first act of life is your mothers embrace. Every diaper changing, feeding, and lullaby sung to you reassures that love. You understand the feeling because it's our most natural action.

Love reaches back. It reciprocates. We know of no evil until one day another child snatches a toy from us. You snatch it back or you cry. How did you know the toy was yours? It never crossed your mind until someone took it from you.

Now that I've made my case, let me ask you.... Do you feel that you have been desensitized by too many traumatic events in society? Are you part of the social media obsession with hate and critique? Has it become too easy for you to hate? Why do you hate? Who do you hate? Do you even know why?

I'm sure you have to hate something. It's the way of the world. Who is it? The skinny girl at work with model looks? A former friend who's dating your ex - boyfriend? Your boss? Husband? Wife? Who? What's so wrong with love?

Whoever or whatever it is - let it go! You will never reach your full potential in life with hate clinging to your spirit. Hate destroys the heart. It's especially wrong to hate happy people. I've heard it before; "why the hell are you so happy?" Why does being happy require an explanation?

Besides, some people who appear happy are really not happy at all. They probably assume you're happy too. You are happy right? A recent survey placed The United States 15th in terms of happiness. Yeah - number 15!

How are we 15th? The most wealthy, opportunistic, and freest country on the planet #15? That must be wrong! Well, it has the top issue affecting our happiness as lack of social support. That's feeling like no one's there! Selfish Americans even messing up the happiness ranking.

The challenge is yours.... Love more. Re-sensitize yourself, if that's even a word. I challenge you to resist negative thoughts, comments, posts, tweets, and actions. Religious hate, gender hate, race hate, or any other kind of hate is outdated.

Love your family. Lafamilia is forever! My grandmother in Baltimore was a soulful woman. Her mother was West Indian, her father Italian (shout out to Levroni). She was the cornerstone of the family. Everybody called her Mama. Life gives us much time to heal family issues. To correct things with family. Pick up the phone and call. Forgive! Love is more powerful than hate. Stop and just think for a moment. Do you really hate your mother? Why? Can you forgive her? Stop being in pride. Pride is the enemy of love. Pride destroys the foundation that love rests on. You can get pass all that if you just stop, think, and pray. Again - forgive! Just step outside of what you feel, and imagine how they must feel.

One more thing.....stop trippin off social media! That whole thing is whack, if you let it run you. Life is not meant to be lived behind a screen.

True living is in front of those you love. It's felt in moments and thoughts of simplicity. It's the air we breathe and touches of kindness. The hippies were on to something.... The weed and promiscuous behavior, drowned out the real message. - LOVE! Attention to your feelings

Make sure you are in touch with your soul. Don't let them people on T.V. fool you. They show you chaos to make your spirit chaotic. To dull your senses. Hopefully I woke you up. Welcome to the movement.

Love 17'

Quote me....

We do not chose to be born. We do not choose our parents. We do not choose our historical epoch, the country of our birth, or the immediate circumstances of our upbringing... But within the realm of choicelessness, we do choose how we live.

Joseph Epstein

5

Inner City Blues

President Trump and Attorney General Jeff Sessions, are both in agreement to end the federal receivership program enacted by President Obama. Federal receivership is aimed at police departments, to encourage accountability with investigations against the department. Kind of like a big brother to ensure policies and procedures are followed. Given the recent climate of police brutality, why would our President and Attorney General agree to dismiss such a measure??? What kind of message does that send the police departments? Where does this leave the trust for law enforcement, inside of our inner cities, where cases of brutality are rampant?

The most symbolic song ever wrote for the hood is Marvin Gaye's "Inner City Blues." My opinion of course. Pull it up and listen to Marvin moaning the chorus "makes me wanna hollar, throw up both my hands!" The infliction of pain dancing in unison across Marvin's tongue. Listen as Marvin harmonizes the perplexities of the hood, city, block, trap, and boroughs.

As a child, I can remember walks with my dad straight down Rhode Island Avenue headed uptown. The smell and the ambiance of the city intoxicating! There's a seduction that releases an allure that at times are irresistible. There's no place you'd rather be. I felt that as early as 8 years old.

My block on Rhode Island Avenue was like a small world to me. On one block you had 3 liquor stores, a lounge, fish market, 3 corner stores, a laundromat, an ice cream parlor, and a funeral home. All on one block.

That's what the hood affords..... convenience! That was the story for the majority of my cousins as well. We were spread out through hoods in PG County Maryland, D.C., and Baltimore. Ice cream trucks, throwback football, girls jumping double-dutch, and fights. You had to know how to fight, because someone would try you.

The major problem with the hood is it's unforgivable. You are never prepared for what's gonna happen - it just happens! A murder, robbery, or whatever - stay on point! You better not be soft cause the city will swallow you up!

The rap group Ghetto Boys had a song in the 90's called "The World is a Ghetto." I started to notice that truth as I traveled through cities like Charlotte, Cleveland, St. Louis, Albuquerque, Dover, and Indianapolis. The dress and slang different - the pain the same.

The hood speaks in simple terms. It's forced poverty. A 15 year old sister is pregnant. The roaches and rats. It's cold and hot at the same time. It's fried bologna and super sweet Kool-Aid. Slow jams and Martin re-runs on the T.V.. It's a lot of beef and love intertwined.

It's also broken promises. I can't get a job. The little boy upstairs got his new North Face coat taken. Domino's pizza won't deliver after 8:00.

The schools are ran down and the teachers don't care. We fight cause we're bored. We shoot cause you fakin like you tough. We scared of the police. The hood Is everything life shouldn't be and still love.

How can so many components of wrong produce so much love? It's the spirit of the ghetto. There's always hope! Somebody will get that elusive government job. One of the kids will graduate and be accepted to college. A father will be released from prison. His kids will come outside later singing "my dad's home, my dad's home!" The story is ever changing.......

My depiction is honest. Life is difficult in the hood. The gangs, drugs, politics, and survival tactics. Many good people are here. Their reasons for not leaving usually vary. This is also America. We create the music, trends, and lingo, then it funnels to the suburbs.

Looking at the hood from a fishbowl gives it no justice. The 6:00 news can't get you here either. To see it, you have to be in it! Our inner cities are messed up and there's no easy way to fix it. Young people feel trapped here. What's our government to do?

Attorney Jeff Sessions says he wants to "lock us up!" Mr. Sessions' words - not mine. This was during his most recent response when asked about the rise in violent crime. Mr. Sessions even commented that he wants to build more private prisons. This is in spite of the Bureau of prisons population being down 29,000 from 2013-2014. I guess Attorney General Sessions has a plan to fill all those prisons.

Do you know what the plan is? The plan is mass incarceration. Of course this will affect minority men at alarming rates.

President Trump laid the blueprint at his inauguration when he emphasized gangs and drugs. - The fix is in homie!

The inner cities have been stuck in decay since heroines hold in the 70's.

No state of emergency was declared. No mayors, senators, or congressman screaming to help our dads. Many of them came back from Vietnam already addicted. Then before long, it was also some of our mothers chasing *ron*. Ron was a bad man, and still is - even today. The opioid epidemic is attacking all races and classes.

To know the plight of the hood, you must have an accurate narrative. Heroine's cunning force started many of the problems in the hood; but the crack epidemic came and cemented them in stone! Heroine was tough, but crack a whole different monster!

I stand firmly by a statement I've made many times over the past 10 years: Crack cocaine is the single worst thing to ever happen to inner cities. - It destroyed it!

Crack made people you've known all your life become unrecognizable in appearance and actions. We called it "crack head moves." Those are the things crack addicts would do to get a rock. Nothing and no one else would matter! So the term crackhead was born.

Heroine could not compare to crack. Heroine had our dads missing, while crack had our moms and dads missing. It happened over night literally. Crack ran the streets and Ronald Reagan finally paid attention. Well, he sent Nancy as his surrogate with the message, "crack is whack!"

In the DC and Maryland area, we had a show called "City Under Siege". City Under Siege chronicled cracks early days from a street perspective. It was cutting edge and real! City Under Siege documented the violence, corruption, and despair of cracks influence. You'd be hard pressed to find a family without at least one crack addict.

As for the cities themselves, they rolled with the punches. Young minority men cashed in. The hood became transfixed by expensive foreign cars and designer clothes. Young men coming from nothing, who suddenly felt like royalty. Young women sporting Louis Vuitton, MCM, and Gucci handbags. Money was everywhere!

With all of this new money, came an increased amount of power. Power that 16, 17, and 18 year olds knew nothing about. Dudes making $10,000 a week, but was just eating fruit loops and sleeping on grandma's sofa. The power was too seductive to pass up. Friends started killing each other. You could see someone at 3:00 in the afternoon smiling bright and by 9:00 that night - he was dead!

The late 80's was hell for inner cities....

Then one evening 60 Minutes came with an interview. THEE interview. The voice prompt said "how did this man become the most powerful drug kingpin in America, right from our Nations' Capital?" I knew it was Rayful.......

Rayful Edmonds lll was considered Americas' first introduction to the inner city drug kingpin. Rayful was clear evidence of what Pablo's cocaine fad done to America. A young black man with enough money and influence to be the lead story on 60 Minutes.

The estimates have Rayful making $30,000,000 a month. Profits that were not the results of luck. Rayful was charismatic with a penchant for math and organization. Rayful established a connect straight from L.A. to lower his buy price. With connect in tow, Rayful was able to supply 90% of the D.C. metropolitan area with cocaine. Let me put this in lament terms; Rayful was a God on the streets of D.C.

The interview on 60 minutes showed it all. The cars, diamond encrusted watches, and limitless amounts of money. They spoke on his $100,000 shopping sprees. They described his way of manipulation through money. How? Buy your whole crew Benzes.

60 minutes labeled Rayful a genius! His teeth were white, and his smile was magnetic. You could feel his control throughout the interview. The nerve of this dude having the brains to acquire such power. Street dudes were not supposed to be that intelligent. Rayful changed the possibilities.

I watched the interview from a crack house in Minneapolis. I'm ashamed now to admit such a thing. That was my life at the time. I knew the story. Even dudes in Minneapolis that I hustled with, knew the story. But the story had more meaning to me, cause I had actually met the "myth". Well, I don't know if anyone would classify the happenstance as we met. You be the judge.......

I'm out in front of Bass liquor store, doing my usual services to the hustlers: grab a bag, wipe a window, throw something away. A BMW pulls up in front of Bass, and the temperature changed. It's a certain aura that attaches to people of influence. When they arrive - all eyes engage. Rayful was in the passenger seat, being chauffeured. All I heard was, "Hey Ray! Hey Ray!" I thought to myself, "how did all these people know who this was?"

I stared in awe as people paid homage with hello's and groupie looks. Many street stars had come through Bass on late nights for a bottle and some snacks. None of them caused this type of raucous. Suddenly he smiled at me, as I stood stuck like molasses with stars marauding in my eyes. He called me over and gave me $100 bill and instructed, "get you some money youngin." The B.M.W. disappeared into the night!

All of this flashed through my cerebral, as I watched the interview. Had that one chance encounter, somehow landed me inside this Minneapolis crack house? Rayful told me to get some money. Now here he was on 60 minutes, almost guaranteed to never see the streets again! He still smiled… memories.

To my surprise, in 1991 Minneapolis had a pretty healthy drug market. Most of the hustlers were migrants from other cities. Men and women hailing from cities like Chicago, Kansas City, Jackson, L.A., Gary, Detroit, and St. Louis. My instinct was a little more polished. Shout out to Monte, Gilbert (RIP) Big Mark, Sade, Chatter Cat, 40 and E Dub.

We were all young and getting money. It happened overnight! It went from riding scooters and rapping in the basement; to cars, clothes, apartments, and women. I was lost inside of the rules governing the game: do good business - no snitching - hustle hard! I would eventually find out that Rayful was snitching. It broke my heart……

As time went on, the despair of crack wore on my spirit. I had witnessed too much devastation. Women who were no longer mothers. Husbands renting out their wives for sexual favors. No matter how in sync I was with the streets, my heart was always soft. While holding my 2 year old daughter in my arms, I gave it up!

Countless stories like this are sequestered inside the concrete of hoods all over America. Men, women, mothers, and fathers who didn't make it out.

Many have died and even more went to prison. The stories documented in Fed cases and newspaper articles.

There have been many Rayfuls since then.... Crack is still sold on streets throughout the country. Heroine has returned, and is alive and well. The wounds are still fresh. The repercussions on family's still undetermined. How can you estimate cracks damage?

People in the hood feel forgotten about. Liquor stores on every corner. Schools and housing projects eroding. Drugs and guns way too accessible. This is the ghetto that Marvin sang about. (Hang ups, let downs, bad breaks, set backs..).

Where's the help at? We send aid to Iraq and let our fellow Americans suffer. Where are the corporate sponsors and billion dollar companies? These same entities profit heavily from money spent in the hood. We buy food, clothes, cars, jewelry, furniture, cosmetics, cell phones, and more. Pepsi, McDonalds, Sony, Nike, Gucci, etc......

I thought President Obama would of done more, but he ran right into a recession his first day in office. Trump has spoken several times about the poor conditions of the inner cities, but we'll see if he does anything,

Poverty rates are staggering. Single parent households debilitating. Alcohol and drug abuse stats off the charts! Our children are stuck inside a quagmire. Does America really care?

As I stated earlier, we will never get to the bottom of how heroine, coke, and guns got into our inner cities. We are clear however on the results: addiction, poverty, murders, downtrodden schools, broken families, and long prison sentences. It's all messed up! It's gonna take the whole Nation to fix it. It's in our best interest morally, socially, and financially to fix it. Our tax dollars are paying for the prisons, healthcare, welfare, and all the other fees associated with systemic failures of our inner cities.

Before I go any further, let me take a second to confront the unsympathetic people. The ones who say, "oh, people need to get up off their butts and work!" Or, here's my favorite: "we all get the same chance in life". Well, until you come from astute poverty, please don't speak on its opportunities. To be poor and underserved is a daunting task. Feeling like nobody feels your pain.

Those are enormous odds.

Here's what I feel is the course of action to quell some of the conditions. It's a 5 point plan in brief. It would take another book to break it down completely.

#1 Education: For people of impoverished areas to do better, the education has to be better! Many inner city schools lack the equipment, incentives and motivations of suburban schools. We have to endorse Science, Technology, Engineering, Math.(S.T.E.M.)

With proper education, people can beat the odds of poverty. One important factor: We have to pay our teachers fairly. Would you want to teach worrying about your bills?

#2 Restore families: Every child needs two parents to develop all the tools needed in life. The inner cities need more family counseling and parenting programs. Many black men grew up without fathers so in turn, it's difficult being a father. You have no example to draw from. A more complete family translates into better communities.

#3 Substance abuse and mental health treatment: The effects of alcohol and drug abuse has been lying dormant for years. We drink and get high to get by. Today, its spice, high grade weed, pills, P.C.P., and molly. People have to believe that they can relate without substances. Listen closely for a second....

The mental health crisis is paralyzing our inner cities. Many people in the inner cities have no idea they have mental health issues. Mental health is the silent bully in the hood. Nobody wants to express internal issues. It's considered soft and uncool. Nobody wants to be vulnerable in such a hard environment. It's going to take the brightest minds in psychology, psychiatry, rehabilitation, and sociology. It will take care, concern, and compassion.

#4 Heath and Wellness: There's no guide book for nutrition and dietary needs in the hood. We're eating Cheetos and drinking Pepsi's. Many of us know nothing about calories, protein, carbs, or sugars. Our family genetics are rich in high blood pressure, diabetes, and heart disease. Our ancestors ate the pig to survive! First Lady Michelle Obama, started a wonderful initiative for our children in school. That will not erase centuries of dietary ignorance. We need qualified nutrition and fitness experts. Where's Doctor Oz when you need him?

#5 Life Training: People in the hood need REAL life training. Help us learn money. Give us assistance on career choices. These things can keep us out of prison. We need comprehensive life training labs in our inner cities. A place where people can get information on topics ranging from credit ratings, employment networking, to proper work attire. Life training labs is the key. We can get volunteers to assist: College students, professionals, bankers, etc..... What if each person had one hour a day to donate. Just one hour! That hour could even be by fielding phone calls from Life Training participants.

The small things matter in a fight this prolific. We are truly fighting for lives! People will change if they have the information on how. This simple 5 point plan could change the lives of millions! A plan mixed with a little bit of money, and a little bit of time. We should have no issue with neither one of those, because the ghetto provides a lot of money, and we've done a lot of time.

A lot of people in the hood feel used. As soon as a corporation wants to come in, they start pushing people out. It's happening in DC right now. The politically correct word is GENTRIFICATION.

"We need this neighborhood to make money - move!"

Hopefully this short synopsis will start a conversation. Please don't forget about our inner cities, hoods, and ghettos. It's as American as apple pie. Many of our celebrities ascended from there: Kanye, Jennifer Lopez, Denzel Washington, Jay-Z, Beyonc'e', Mark Wahlberg, Jennifer Hudson, Kendrick Lamar, Lebron James, Alicia Keys, 50 cent, and more. All of them maybe not from the hood - hood, but they know the truths!

The task itself can seem insurmountable, but it's possible! We as a team can do it, one computer lab at a time; one teacher, one volunteer, one book club, one donation, one idea. Patience is the key to this endeavor. We can't leave it like this? How can a true American, leave a part of America suffering? If one part of the body is infected, the whole body is at risk!

May the late great Marvin Gaye rest in peace. Very few since Marvin, have been able to deliver the inner city blues in such vividness. I pray for peace in the hoods all over America. If nobody else feels you - I do! I spoke for you, and will continue to do so every chance I get. Now you gotta do your part.

Quote me.......

The world is before you, and you need not take it or leave it as it was when you came in.

- James Baldwin

6

Such is Life (The Ills)

Jimmy Kimmel gave a monologue totally devoted to his newborn son. While fighting back tears, Jimmy spoke on the battle his son had at birth with a heart defect. He then thanked the many doctors and nurses who completed a successful surgery on the newborn. Jimmy then pleaded for lawmakers to pass a legitimate healthcare bill that will assist ALL families with healthcare. Jimmy stated that no family should be denied emergency or lifesaving medical care due to financial reasons. They 'listened, hence the sloppy - quick bill. Welcome to the ills......

My Aunt Diane is currently in a fight with cancer. My Aunt Polly just concluded a bout with cancer - she won! My wife has friends and family fighting cancer as we speak. All of them women.

It seems like cancer has a prejudiced grip on women. I do hear cases of men having colon, prostate, or leukemia, but it seems like women are at odds with the disease. My aunts are in real fights with cancer and I pray for them daily. This is where real faith in God steps in.

Both aunts braved mastectomy procedures. Aunt Polly appears to have a clean bill of health. Aunt Diane's fight has been a little more difficult. After a period of recovery post chemotherapy, the cancer appeared in other parts of her body. She will not be moved! This loving and caring woman is like a mother to me. It's not right!!! Do you care if I cry as I write this chapter to you? You'll never see my tears. All you'll feel is the weight of my words. Women are carrying the weight of cancer on their shoulders. Just like they carry the weight of the family. I recently told my wife that I think there's a connection. What if the never ending stress of work, family, nurturing, and sacrifice, was somehow making women more vulnerable to the disease?

As my wife constantly reminds me, "the body is very sensitive". - Welcome to the balancing act of women! The wife who cooks; the mother who gets the kids off to school; the sister who's there to give advice; the daughter available to care take.; and the friend ready to organize the next event. WOMEN.

The fight against cancer rages on. We MUST be more involved. It WILL affect you or someone you know at some point. Just wearing pink throughout the month of October is not enough. We need answers! This fight has to be 24 hours a day, 365 days a year. The men, women, and children fighting need us.....

A lot of money has been donated. Progress has been made. However, this disease is still too powerful! Early detection is vitally essential to the fight.

Shout out to Aunt Diane and Aunt Polly. Also a special shout out to all the victims and survivors of cancer. I will tell your story. Keep fighting! We will do the research and become more aware. The American Cancer Society and many other organizations are a phone call away. The more we know - the more we can help!

Such is life, is a chapter dedicated to confronting life's ills. I started with cancer because it's always there. Did you notice, or are you sleep? Put down your cell phone and power off the IPad. Wake up! Life is moving with all kinds of challenges attached. Heart disease, diabetes, high blood pressure, Parkinson's, Alzheimer's, and more. The ills are real!

Global warming is one of the ills. It was deathly hot last summer. I'm talking that, "damn it feels like Vegas type heat". The experts have verified that 2016 was the hottest year on record - EVER! Winter did not feel like winter at all. Are you woke yet? Put the cell phone down.

The Associated Press (AP) recently published a report (March 2007) about the Arctic sea ice. The A.P. reported that arctic sea ice has dipped to a record level. The Arctic ice level is a key part of Earth's climate system. Less ice on the Artic, translates into hotter than normal temperatures. It also will keep those hot temperatures around for prolonged periods of time. So it could easily be 90+ degrees for 2-3 weeks straight!

Here's some good news..... The Associated Press, recently reported that China and India, are leading in worldwide cutbacks on the construction of new coal fired power plants. That's good news but we still have a HUGE problem....

Our problem is President Trump! He recently signed an executive order, going against all progress America was making against global warming.

President Trump claims it was a move to create jobs for coal miners. That's garbage! It was actually a shot at President Obama for whom Trump dislikes for his own precarious reasons.

Are you woke now? I'm trying to get you away from Instagram, Facebook and Twitter. The earth is way too hot! The jet stream is way out of sync. This is causing crazy weather patterns, wildfires, floods, tornadoes, heat waves, and dangerous storms. Stop sleeping on this!

Global warming is not science - its reality!

The ills of life will never go away. The earth has been tested and threatened since the beginning of time. Earth has endured many catastrophes, man-made poisons and more. That does not mean the Earth doesn't have feelings. So if you've got one environmentalist bone in your body - get involved!

Let's shift gears for a second to another one of life's ills..... HIV/AIDS. A lot of people are believing a rumor that a cure exists somewhere. Sorry to break the bad news to you - no cure! The money is in the medication - not the cure!

If all the ills had a cure, what would the researchers, drug makers, and doctors do? The money is in treatment. As a researcher, do I really want a cure to be found? That negates the billions of dollars poured into the research.

There's always gonna be a SARS, West Nile Virus or Zika. If all of us were healthy, where would that put the health industry? Health care is the biggest racket in the world! All the money is in the preparation to die. So eat that greasy burger, smoke a cigarette, and start preparations.

Let's go back to HIV/ AIDS for a moment.... A lot of us are still dancing with death. Still not wearing rubbers? Choosing lust over life!

Magic Johnson announced he had HIV in 1991. You can still catch Magic at Lakers games, where he is currently working in management. Magic looks wonderful over 25 years later. Magic is also worth over a half billion dollars. His access to medical treatment and medication is different than yours.

I know three people who died from AIDS, one of them a cousin. My wife knows of people also. Most of the cases involving normal people, lead to a lonely hospital room with IV's, tubes, and despair. We usually label it pneumonia until they die.

No matter your lifestyle - get on point! Protect yourself at all times. You never want to put yourself in a position to suffer. Research shows people living g decades after their HIV diagnosis. Some people die quick from the virus. Don't be one of the few that wakes up in that small hospital room, telling everybody you got pneumonia. The HIV virus is real! There's no Magic cure...

Many of our ills are not physical. Our ills can range from emotional, social, political, familial, and more. You have to be aware of them cause they can affect your quality of life.

I want to stir you, shake you, move you, provoke you, challenge you, and inspire you. The small books singular mission is to put life in front of you and let you process it. I'm not trying to scare you - I love you! I want you aware and poised to your world.

The next thing I want to do is speak on some social ills. These have been around for years and the cause of much debate. I am not at liberty to say who is right of wrong, I only choose to give you my opinion. You may agree or disagree with my opinion, but at least you will be involved. Let's go....

Abortion

I have been hearing about the abortion issue for most of my life. Roe versus Wade, abortion clinic violence, and Supreme Court decisions. I've heard from conservatives, liberals, religious groups, men, women, and other casual proponents.

It is one of the most sensitive issues of our time. People have voted for presidents to gain leverage and influence on the issue. Presidents have nominated Supreme Court judges in hopes of footing on shaping abortion.

Whether prolife or prochoice, we all know this cause. I myself have done much flip flopping on the issue. When I was a young man in the streets, there was a commonality to abortions. I don't know if that's a hood thing - that's just how it was. I even supported the decision twice, to abort pregnancies that I had caused. We both agreed it was not the right time. Prochoice!

As I got older and more spiritually grounded, my convictions became stronger on abortion. "How could a woman do that to a fetus?" There had to be other options. I was a pessimist to the highest order. Prolife!

Then one day I was watching a documentary on PBS about rape victims who choose abortions. For that moment I stepped out of myself and into the shoes of that woman. What if it was rape? What about incest? What if the mother was a crack addict? All of these questions ran through my mind.

So after much internal debate and soul searching, I stand today as a prochoice supporter. That choice does not come without regret. I do feel that it's the right decision though. I have no right regardless of my religious beliefs, to tell a woman what to do with her body. I would not try to convince someone else to change their beliefs. It's a tough choice. I say now, after much consideration - prochoice.

* The Death Penalty *

Arkansas is preparing to execute 8 people over a 10 day period. Two executions are scheduled for April 17th, April 20th, April 24th, and April 27th. Arkansas Governor Asa Hutchinson, has been questioned repeatedly over the past few weeks about so many executions in such a short period of time. The stressful impact possibly imposed on medical staff and prison officials. Governor Hutchinson quotes the Arkansas Department of Corrections director as saying, "all medical staff and prison officials are trained for this."

I don't know if anybody trains to see 8 executions in 10 days. That's going beyond the call of duty! There has to be an emotional strain dealing with so much death in a short span. The reasoning for so many executions so quick? - The anesthesia used is due to expire soon. The company that provides the anesthesia is against the death penalty, and will not provide more.

I don't know what these 8 men did to be facing execution. I am sympathetic to the victims and their families. However, I firmly believe that God is the only one with a right to end a life. I cannot say when or where someone should die.

I do understand how a loved one could feel vindicated by seeing the death penalty administered. I can't imagine what kind of pain has to be felt to request such retribution.

My stance is against the death penalty. In my eyes, God and God alone has the right to give and take life. I have taken into account the heinous acts that could warrant death, but who am I? As a Christian I believe that vengeance belongs to God. May you respect my position.

Gun control

The N.R.A. are some bad people. They are the ultimate bully's. The most powerful political organization there is. The N.R.A. is not really a political organization, but there influence always affects politics. As long as the N.R.A. has a hat in the arena, gun control will stall.

The violent acts of Sandy Hook hurt me to my heart.

To imagine elementary school children facing such horror is too much for me. I never in my life thought that a Sandy Hook was possible! At least spare the kids. I knew for a fact that this would be the reason for more meaningful gun legislation. Boy was I wrong!

The initial response was overwhelming. President Obama gave some real heartfelt remarks while shedding tears. Politicians pledging to cross party lines and work together. I thought we had something. Or so I thought!

Out of nowhere came the grumblings of the NRA. They played nice at first immediately following Sandy Hook - but the tone quickly changed. Some of the language being spoken by lawmakers didn't sit well with the NRA. They shot back! "Guns don't kill people, people kill people." I thought to myself, "these people really love their guns." That's some weird stuff! Kids died and the fight for guns continue.

How could any red blooded human being not be disgusted by Sandy Hook? That same disgust would make any sane human being want to do something to ensure this never happens again. That's what it should be about! Why would we wanna keep waking up to breaking news that pierces the soul? It slowly leeches away at all the things that give us hope.

To still fight tooth and nail even after Sandy Hooks events, showed me exactly how far the National Rifle Association would go to win. I saw it with my own eyes, and our coward ass politicians fell right in line. Now it's like Sandy Hook never happened. And y'all are not weird? Yeah right!

I stand firmly in belief that we need gun control. I know who these guns have been killing other than the mass shooting victims.

I gave you the game in Chapter Four: Love/Hate. Guns are killing black and brown men, and have been for decades. That's who've really carried the burden of no gun control.

The wicked realities are coming home to roost. These shootings occur as often as a full moon. Americans are turning on America. Who saw Orlando coming? The D.C. sniper? When will it stop?

Earlier this year (March 2017), Brooklyn had the biggest drug bust in New York City's history. Authorities confiscated 200+ guns from a gun ring. The gun ring consisted of 24 black men ages from 19-34. The men were buying the guns for cheap in Virginia, and selling them for profit in New York. The money was better in New York City because of stricter gun laws.

How in 2017 can 24 young black men buy 200+ guns of all variety and capabilities? Obviously someone does not care! This has nothing to do with the men being black - its period! I don't think 24 young white men should be able to just buy unlimited guns. That's a problem!

The Richmond Times reports the men having ties to the bloods street gang.

Virginia should be ashamed of itself! For me and 24 dudes who look like me, to successfully be able to buy 200 guns is crazy! Our politicians and the NRA (National Rifle Association) should be ashamed.

But oh well, the NRA wants guns - the NRA gets guns.

I fear the day of another Sandy Hook. Another Aurora. Pulse nightclub. Guns are too easy to buy. Unless we push for more accountability from our politicians, these shootings will never stop!

More needs to be done with mental health backgrounds. I believe there should be a mental health questionnaire available when applying to purchase a gun. That in itself may reveal signs of a person having mental health difficulties.

We have a duty to protect ourselves from these random acts of violence. I pray that something can be done. Damn, only if the NRA didn't love their guns so much..........

Quote me...

Change your thoughts and you change your world.

- Norman Vincent Peale

7

The Culture: Drugs, Sex, Politics, and Music

Maybe I've been too soft on Hillary. That loyal democrat in me sparing her any more pain. Well, if I'm going win that Pulitzer, I guess my literary contribution has to be allegiance free. So here we go.... Hillary blew the election. It hurts to say it - but it's true! When you are on a certain level, you can't slip. Your game must be tight! Especially when it comes to electronic threads. That stuff forever exists in cyberspace. As secretary of state, Hillary had to be more on point. I still think she got a bad rap, but that's how the game goes.

You're not running for head of your soccer moms group - this is for President of the United States. All the marbles.

El Chapo & The Donald

You can sum up the jest of American culture with these four words: drugs, sex, politics, and music. Each one creating its own paradigm. This is our culture, whether we choose to believe it or not. You could very well add religion in there, or sports, or even technology, but those are still evolving. Drugs, sex, politics, and music rule! - Welcome to the new world order.

Less than a year ago, the United States extradited Mexican drug lord "El Chapo Guzman" to New York. It was actually the night before President Trumps inauguration. I believe it was a symbolic sign from President Trump to El Chapo, noting their feud during the campaign. Some unflattering comments about Mexicans made by Trump, ticked El Chapo off!

El Chapos extradition to the U.S. is supposed to immediately make Mexican and American streets more safe and less drug riddled. El Chapo has escaped multiple times from Mexican authorities. His most recent absconding success was from a maximum security cell in Mexico via a underground tunnel. That's influence!

People get high and listen to music. Musicians sing about sex and politics. Politicians get caught in sex scandals - it's all relative! Katy Perry, Lady Ga-Ga, and Rhianna, are not music's first sexual rebels. Even before Madonna, music was always sex's biggest aphrodisiac. Music is played, love is made, babies are born.

Bill Clinton, Elliott Spitzer, Mayor Marion Barry, Governor Schwarzenegger, Anthony Weiner, Clarence Thomas, John Edwards, President J.F.K., Gary Condit, Newt Gingrich, Mark Sanford, and even the now former - Governor Jerry Brown of Alabama. All politicians linked to sex scandal. Well, I guess we can throw in President Trump, and there you have it - sex and politics!

We tend to underestimate the pressures distorting our politicians. These walking, talking, canvasses of power, waiting to be corrupted. I am not conjuring an excuse for them, that's real pressure! Politicians fall blamelessly into the culture by process of elimination.

Music is the one out of the four that exemplifies the culture. Picture this year's 2017 Grammys. The buzz all about 'and Adele. Two musical goliaths battling for music's most prestigious trophies. Americans love trophies.

Adele opened the show with "hello" in perfect tune. Beyonc'e had a memorable performance with bare stomach exposed, celebrating her pregnancy with twins. Bey's tone angelic. But the night belonged to Adele. Upon winning the biggest awards of the night, Adele thanked Beyonc'e in a fashion that appeared as genuine as genuine offers. Tears flowed, twitter went crazy, and that's music!

Music has the discernment to unite and humble even multiple Grammy winners. Music is always there: it's played at weddings, funerals, birthdays, Bar Mitzvahs, churches, and sporting events. It's even caressing my ears now as I write this to you.(Lalah Hathaway)

Music is the greatest uniting force ever! Chuck Berry, The Beatles, Elvis, Janis Joplin, Ray Charles, Chubby Checker, Little Richard, Hendrix, and so many others gave us cross over. Cross over just a code word for uniting.

I grew up hearing the critics say, Elvis stole rock n roll. Black folks really perpetuated this conspiracy. Chuck Berry (may he rest in peace) has commented over the years that rock n roll was never his. Little Richard however, carried a much different opinion. He affectionately called himself the "Originator".

In my opinion, music can never be owned. It's an element of free expression. You can own your masters true enough. But the inspiration will forever be drawn from. Music as is religion, belongs to no one!

Sex, sex, sex, sex! It seems like women are half naked everywhere. Whether a commercial for Carl Jr's, organic milk, or cars. It's all about the sex appeal and exposure.

Rhianna comes on stage with a see through top breasts exposed. Nicki Minaj stomps on stage with her butt cheeks out. The crowd goes wild! Madonna, Janet, and Brittany all had their moments in the sexual spot light. This is the culture......

Porn is being consumed at an all- time high. Escort services, internet sex sites, and kinky web sites are rolling out every day. People are now into swinging, voyeurism, and fetishes. One of the nets most popular sites is "seeking arrangement." Seeking arrangement translates into, wealthy men looking for younger women to please them socially, egotistically, or physically. Young college women are flocking to the site to ease the burdens of tuition.

Politicians are constantly being courted by lobbyists. The insurance companies, gun makers, environmentalists, conservationists, and drug makers. Americans want drugs, and politicians have no good reason to stop them. Money talks and prescription drugs keep flowing......

Many states are experiencing an opioid abuse crisis. The overdoses keep happening, and the ideas are getting low.

An Ohio pilot and his wife overdosed earlier this year. Investigators found fentanyl in their home. Drugs have no face and no class! Politicians are scrambling to pass legislation to fund states war on opioid abuse.

Even as El Chapo sits inside his new American cell, drugs are crossing the border. (Trump better hurry up with that wall.) Business must go on. What will the wall do about the tunnels, speedboats, private planes, human stomachs, and hidden car compartments? Americans want it - Mexico will get it here.

*music's responsibility and bad politics *

I grew up loving music. Michael Jackson, Prince, Stevie Wonder, Bee Gees, Fleetwood Mac, and more! If the sound was right, it was right! Music soothes the soul....

I truly believe that our musicians should carry more responsibility for the ills of the world. A microphone and stage carries a lot of leverage. It can't just be Katy Perry, Kendrick Lamar, Beyonc'e, Common, and Chance the rapper.

We need more voices. I am not saying every musician has to speak out, but we need more!

I understand the politics (more politics) of sponsorship and endorsements. For many, that's how they pay the bills. Who wants to lose money? But if you know the truth - you gotta speak on it! If your fans are with you, they'll be with you regardless. Don't etch your legacy in money, solidify with lyrics. Your words. That's what changes hearts!

Politicians have been *bullshitting* the American people for all my life. Minimum wage is too low; taxes too high; our schools are bad; healthcare marginal; and social security garbage. The list is long, and I haven't even gotten to the infrastructure and other issues.

Billions of dollars change hands every year. My wife recently vented to me about all the money being taken out of her check each payday. I tried to quell her frustrations to no avail.

It's a joke! The HBO political show "The Circus" is fitting.

Since President Trump has taken office, he has waged war against immigration, tried to impose a travel ban, and went after Obamacare. Well, if you consider the rushed alternative that President Trump and the republicans rolled out. There were so many holes in the plan, that even fellow republicans couldn't support it. Healthcare is too important to be rushed out of spite.

The next issue is President Trumps proposed budget. Billions of dollars in increased military spending. Drastic cuts to Medicaid, arts/humanities, housing, and infrastructure. So many cuts to social programs that it's almost like Trump saying, "okay, so what if you're struggling - take care of yourself."

Why such an increase in military spending? What war are we getting ready for? Certainly not with his friends in Russia. Just piggy backing on the friendship award that Rex Tillerson received from Russia.

No need in being surprised, this is politics! Politicians take their own ideals and press them upon the American people. Seen the new tax code yet? All cuts for the elite among us.

Let me point out the thing that stands out the most to me..... Trump proposes to reduce the seven tax brackets from seven to three. Let me translate that for you fight quick: #1 Rich #2 Almost poor #3 Poor That's really how it will break down.

Do you know who I feel sorry for? Those non educated rural white men who won it for Trump. Nothing in the tax code for them.

President Trump is now pushing a new healthcare plan. One that he says will cover pre-existing conditions and produce lower premiums. That budget I spoke on, is also being tweaked. Right now the focus is on North Korean leader Kim Jong Un- - so I'll keep you posted!

quick sex-music's message - Obama

The speed at which men and women can find sexual partners these days, is astonishing! Dating sites like "Tinder" is currently offering hook ups. You stroll through until you find an attractive photo. You send a message and see if they wanna hook up. If so, you could be having sex soon. So much for the old date at 8.

Women are but objects now. I often mentor younger guys on their perceptions of women. What they tell me is complexed. Its women at their disposal to be slept with. No work, no wooing, - just hook up sex! Because if one won't, another one will......

These perceptions have been psychologically fed to us from media outlets. The Bachelor, Flava of Love, Temptation Island, and many others. One guy and twenty women clawing for him.

As the show goes on, the competition gets more serious. Leaving poor Tiffany at home in Cleveland wondering if she has to do all that to get a man.

This is what our culture of sex has given us. It has created this microcosm of relationship discord. Relations have abandoned the relationship theory.

Many people believe that relationships are becoming extinct. The experts and surveys have spoken loudly. Steve Harvey has even wrote some books to help. But the reality still remains: smart, confidant, down to earth woman, looking for a man. Well, the profile would go something like that.

I can remember late nights riding home with Tupac playing in my speakers. Of course I was much younger then, but Pac was spewing the realities of my life. Describing in vivid detail the streets and all of its trappings. The rawness of "The White Manz World." His mother Afeni, a Black Panther, so truth was his genetically.

Music and politics are interchangeable parts. Bob Dylan and Paul Simon are two of the most prolific writers in history. Listen to Bob Dylan singing, "Times are a changing." The grasp of his voice relays the contempt of time at that moment. As if you're watching life unfold in his lyrics. The closest to PAC today in my eyes is Kendrick Lamar.

I've begun to understand why the republicans hated Obama so much..... He came in and messed up the money! President Obama held banks accountable for ridiculous fee strife interest rates on loans. He went after Wall Street with regulations much needed. Then he pissed off the old insurance companies, with the affordable care act. Obama must have lost his mind, messing up establishment dough!

But seriously, President Obama inherited the job with America in its worse state since the great depression.

The housing market crashed; unemployment confusingly high; the automobile industry amuck in debt. President Obama looked all of that in the face, and went to work!

Look where we stand eight years later.... People are buying homes, unemployment is under 4%, and interest rates are low. Oh, and the stock market is over 20,000 points! President Trump can't take credit for none of that. He has to at least have a year in.

So how can I do the culture with politics involved, and not salute President Obama. He and first lady Michelle Obama were class and grace for eight years. He stood in the fire and made progress. He did it without scandal tied to his name.

It will be decades before America can put into retrospect what President Obama accomplished. Even how he's handled himself among the Trump birther and wire-tapping allegations. Politics are dangerous dear reader - don't be fooled! President Obama was a solid POTUS.

*predators, drugs, and music mortality *

Children have become the new face of sex. Whether in big cities or small towns, adults are being charged with crimes against children. Many in possession of child pornography, others accused of sexual abuse of a child. Some are teachers, pastors, coaches, and other trusted adults. We are not properly protecting our children. (* 4.5 million children are missing in America*)

Right now in Washington D.C., children are being reported missing every day. Some theorists believe the children are being snatched by sex traffickers. This is no different than in other cities all over the country. Politicians are numb as usual. This is what our culture if sex has gotten us! It has removed the limitations and boundaries on participants.

When a husband and wife conspires to acquire porn- - something is wrong!

The constant disabuse of sexual images on individuals psyche, begins to deplete the healthy rationale of acceptable behavior.

The FBI locked Jared up, who was infamous for his Subway commercials for losing weight. Jared was in possession of child porn, and also accused of sexual abuse.

The culture of sex in America, has always been lenient on child violators. Administrators at Penn State University failed to act, when information surfaced of alleged abuse by school employee Jerry Sandusky, against a young boy. Prestige over took protection!

I can remember the exact moment when I realized how powerful drugs were. I'm watching some grainy video breaking on the news. A man seemingly undoing something in a room. Then it hit me what was going on....... It was Mayor Marion Barry smoking crack! I was shocked and amazed. How could this happen?

That's the true power of drugs. So many people are using them. Normal everyday people, and even the stars. As the stars shared drug use with its fans, those fans felt enabled. Lil Wayne sips syrup and smokes weed - so can I.

Now you got teenagers and young adults, taking designer drugs. Popping pills which are cheap to buy. They're also smoking high grade weed, snorting coke, and shooting heroine. These are city and suburban kids alike. It's probably your kid, tricking you as if nothing is wrong. Be aware! Who your child is when they walk out that door, differs from the person you see opening the refrigerator.

I smoked weed late into my teenage years. My mother had no idea until it was too late. I had my time though rolling blunts and eating snacks afterward.

Now-a-days drugs are being crossed. Here's how it goes..... You pop a pill, smoke some *loud* weed, and sip some syrup. I'm scared just thinking about it. Hello parents, welcome to the culture......

Music is always evolving. Bruno Mars, The Weekend, Bryson Tiller, Kierra Sheard, Pentatonix, Byron Cage, Fifth Harmony, Lukas Graham, and others are pushing music further. Music is soft, edgy, forceful, and brave. We all have our tastes and preferences. Music will never leave us, only continuing through the pantheons of immoralism.

Music has also left many "what ifs" in its path. Those who left us way too early: Jimi Hendrix, Kurt Cobain, Frankie Lymon, Tupac, Biggie, Whitney, John Lennon, Marvin, Michael, Prince, Amy Winehouse, and many others. Did they reach their creative apex? How are we to know? Gone too early. Many through the abuse of substances.

* The Political Process Challenged. *

Politics will remain "politics", until you decide to change it! You turn over your life, to people you don't even know, without any accountability. Lawmakers decide your healthcare, taxes you pay, your retirement, and even the quality of your children's education. These people blueprint your life - and you're not involved?

You cannot inject yourself into the process every four years, and think you're doing something. - It's not enough! The President is only one person, all of the other elections for Senate and Congress is serious! The midterm elections is where the change comes from.

I am sure that most of my tone throughout the book, pits me as a staunch democrat. That's not true! I identify as democrat in regards to fairness and social issues. I identify as American, in regards to right and wrong. I am not anti - Trump. I just want politicians to do right!

Whoever presents the best agenda - count me in! I agreed with many of Bernie Sanders views on the campaign trail. I was just unsure if he could win it all. So I rode with Hillary until the final bell.

My father taught me how to read the Washington Post at 5 years old. All of those years reading and following politics, has taught me a lot. I have become a master detector of political jargon, white wash, and undertones. Like for instance; I think speaker of the house Paul Ryan, is a genuine person. The problem is, he's aligned with a party of wealthy agendas I don't trust!

I am telling you now, our political system is broken! If we as Americans don't take it back, future generations will pay the cost. We can't take it back by spitefully voting for the first Donald Trump. That comes along. Any elected leader, especially for the presidency, should have some experience in public office. Just not enough experience that they've become complacent and entitled.

You take it back by doing your homework. Research the voting records of those who interest you. You have the right to know how they voted on issues important to you. Here's key piece of advice to you regarding politicians. Do not judge them by what they say, but by what they do!

Don't listen to the talk - go to the record. But for now, be very concerned about President Trump and his need for BIG military. Be very concerned.......

The Culture: drugs, sex, politics, and music

Old Fashion Love

There's no quick fix, to how we view sex in America. The movies, videos, and television shows, will keep on showing it. Feeding your sub - conscious images. Not just your sub - conscious, but our children's as well. So if you're not gonna wage a war against the FCC, I suggest you educate yourself and those around you. The facts are there: the over saturation of sex, social media hook ups, and negative portrayals of women, is killing the process of marriage. Squandering the potential of traditional family's. Men are being given too many reasons to devalue women.

I'm gonna keep these closing words on sex simple.... Real conversations need to be had. Conversations from women with other women. Women need to have conversations with men. Husbands, fathers, brothers, friends, etc....The guidelines have to be re - set on how men look at you, and how you demand they look at you. Each woman must raise the standard cause its bad right now!

The dating scene has drastically changed in 20 years. The countless singles flocking to internet dating sites, has tarnished the human feel of love. We are becoming but a face and a profile. I can encourage you to try meeting people again organically.

Have that conversation. Go to a movie. Sit on the phone for hours, and unfold each other's lives. Bond. Commit. Sex will then curtail a new meaning. To my men: women are more than objects to please us. Real intimacy cannot be embraced through tweets and texts. Change the culture!

This Is Your Brain On Drugs

I believe I've said enough about drugs throughout this book. It affected my father and uncles. It hurt my community. Street legends have been made; aka` Big Meech and The BGF family running Atlanta in the early 2000's. I have been open and very honest with you. I signed up for this!

The drug culture moves on through 2017, like a well oiled machine. El Chapo is not a fictional character. Univision is currently running a series every Sunday night depicting his life. I wonder how many youngsters watching, are being influenced by the lore. Joaquin Guzman Loera is real! He once operated the most extensive Mexico to America drug operation ever contrived.

The illegal drug trade is a $300 billion dollar a year operation worldwide. Tunnels from Mexico to America are still pumping. There will be another Pablo, Rayful, Meech, and El Chapo.

From Sinaloa Mexico, to Concord North Carolina, American hopes are spoiling inside of rigorous addictions. So much has been lost to addiction, trade, and pursuit of drugs. People you know, and people I know. More money and programs are needed.

This thing is real! This is not Matt Lauer featuring Martha Stewart, on the Today show. No cookie cooking here! This is Walter White "Breaking Bad." This is the culture, and I'm just the messenger......

Quote me.....

God pitying the toils which our race is born to undergo, gave us the gift of song.

- Plato

8

"Rich Friends- Poor Enemies"

As a child, I use to ride the train on days I was out of school. From Rhode Island avenue station to Montgomery County. I would watch the environment change. From trash polluted city streets, to the lush greens of Bethesda. The oversized houses and brand new Volvo's, had my young mind California dreaming. The only problem was I had to go back. Back down the red line to the kaleidoscope of the city. The air even smelled different in the burbs. That's about the time I knew the importance of money. That night I'd lay quietly, eyes to the ceiling. All that was on my mind, was those lush greens......

Rich Dad Poor Dad is a comprehensive read for aspiring financial growth seekers. It breaks money down in simple terms. Author Robert Kiyosaki has a very unique way of relaying money terms and principles. Another easy to read book on money is "think and grow rich". Although both books are relatively old publications, the valid points still apply.

That's the weird thing about money. The principles don't change, only the lingo. Finance for dummies: #1 Get a good job #2 Save money and start a 401(k) #3 Build your credit #4 Invest and acquire property #5 Prepare for retirement.

Same game - same rules!

Of course you're saying, "If it's that simple, than why aren't we all rich?" Good question. We all should be rich. Our bank accounts should be stuffed with cash, bubbling IRA's, and diversified portfolios. Not so fast! Rich comes with a process Short cuts are forbidden, with the exception of power ball winners.

After years of studying money and its concepts, I've come to realize two things.....#1 Rich people don't understand poor people #2 Poor people don't trust rich people. Apples and oranges in the scope of ink.

Rich people naturally assume that if you work hard - you too can be rich. While poor people believe rich people were either born that way, or got there through someone opening doors for them. The keep the wealth in the family tactic.

I recently came across a story by a former Washington Post reporter, who experienced wealth and poverty equally. I thought to myself, this would be a great story for this chapter. So after doing some research, I decided to add it respectfully.

The post reporter is named Mr. William McPherson.

Mr. McPherson authored an essay titled, "Falling" Mr. McPherson passed away in 2014, leaving behind this prolific work on privilege and poverty.

In Falling, Mr. McPherson speaks of his youth and dropping out of college. He touches on the many jobs he worked, eventually landing a job at The Washington Post, writing literary criticism. He was awarded a Pulitzer for his work as a reporter. Mr. McPherson also received notoriety for two novels he published. With all the acclaim and awards for his literary contributions, Mr. McPherson gained financial security. He was on top of the world, living his dream! He was in no way prepared to fall.

Mr. McPherson quickly found out that in life, there's no guarantees! Mr. McPherson had the salary, savings, investments, 401(k), pension, and even the retirement. But none of it could save him from his impending doom - Falling!

After some bad decisions and some frivolous spending, Mr. McPherson lost it all! He eventually had no choice but to rely on government assistance. His pride damaged and optimism tested. The essay is eye opening and touching. A man who once held great privilege, facing a reality that millions of Americans endure every day. To be poor....

I never knew we were poor growing up. My mother will probably resent my honesty on his topic, but truth is necessary. My brother and I shared a bed, that became a make shift couch during the day. The brown box government cheese made the best grilled cheese sandwiches. It felt normal....

Summer time temperatures in our apartment were sweltering! Especially if my mother used the oven to cook.

Those nights, I would lay on the kitchen floor with the refrigerator door cracked open to ease my pain. To this day I don't like heat! It still felt normal.....

That's the truth about the rich and the poor- it feels normal! President Trumps' father was a very successful businessman, so his wealth as a child felt normal. Ivanka Trump grew up with a rich dad, so her wealth feels normal.

The principles of money are not taught as extensively to children as it should be.

Some kids are starting out with a poor dad, which already has them behind. So they must be taught earlier about the value of money. It has to be more than adding, subtracting, multiplying, and dividing. Children should have mock stock charts instead of pie charts. If we are going to teach them fractions anyway, let's make it on the stock market. Children will learn money, if we are innovative enough to teach them.

The rich and poor realities are real! It's almost like an old sweater you just can't throw away. As soon as you put it on, it fits you perfectly. That's when you remind yourself to keep it.

The great Tolstoy once commented: "The rich are all alike, but the poor are poor in their own particular ways." The different courses for rich and poor must be discussed. For us to pretend that each side comes without benefits and difficulty would be a lie.

Nobody likes to be called poor, but somebody has to be. From the looks of President Trumps proposed budget, more people will be poor very soon. I don't blame him, he grew up rich. How can he really relate to anything else?

Here in lies the problem with electing a billionaire president.... He really has no grasp of your life's adversities. No matter how many McDonald's hamburgers President Trump eats, identifying with struggling families is hard for him.

But let's not place the blame of wealth or poverty on president Trump.

This divide has been around since Vanderbilt and Rockefeller. Trump only played the hand he was dealt. Wealth and poverty have sinister histories.

To close the gap between rich and poor, one would only have to listen for a moment. It's a matter of ancestry, generational cycles, education, and destination. Rich people enjoy being rich and that's their right. I've never understood however, how poor people sometimes enjoy being poor. Don't be mad at me for saying it - I've seen it!

I watch us waste money on material things. You buy your kids $200 shoes, when you don't have decent savings in the bank. I see 5 year olds in Jordans and True Religion jeans. Stop buying expensive cars before you buy a home. Stop rushing to get your tax refund so you can go spend it on clothes and jewelry.

This message is squarely directed at African Americans......... I will probably get black lash for saying this, but how can I not? How can I stand before you with truth but not divulge it? With all the cute politically correct stuff said, let me get to my views.......

As a member of the African American race I can say without question - we are STUPID WITH MONEY! I been wasting it all my life, and was a participant to the highest degree. Competition for the best while literally being a mess!

We look at the examples of money and try to emulate the path. You can't live like Nicki, Beyonc'e, Future, or Rick Ross. You can't sell enough keys to catch Yo Gotti. Those dudes talk about the trap house, but how many are really in the trap? I sat in those crack house foolishly chasing a dream!

Wake up homie! There's no value in buying cars, clothes, and jewelry. The true value resides with property, investments, and businesses. Trump just cut the corporate tax from 35% to 15%. Money takes care of money!

Welcome to the Da vinci code. We have been chasing ghosts for all our lives. Trying to outdo each other with labels. Have you ever been to fashion week in New York? How about the Met Gala? This year's Met Gala was $30,000 a ticket. The only street dude I saw there was ASAP Rocky. A brother from Harlem who fashion name dropped himself to the biggest night in fashion. But that's the identity of fashion.

On my best dressed night of my life, I had on all Italian labels. From the top of my head to the Ferragamos on my feet. I'm not going to try and estimate the value, it was 20 years ago. When I got home that night to my apartment, I was still dealing with life's issues. That's the reality about labels - you gotta take them off!

This is no knock to my hard working brothers and sisters out there working hard every day. You deserve what you want if you work hard for it. But if you are stretching yourself thin financially for image, you got the game all wrong. True happiness rests in the quality of life, not the quantities. Real money doesn't have to show itself.

We want the biggest weddings, biggest parties, and grand functions.

Stop playing with that money! Before you make any decisions, stop, think, and pray. Ask God to direct your finances. We are not smart enough to make all the best decisions. Ask for wisdom when praying regarding your finances. I am not writing this chapter to worship money.

We are not born to serve money. Money is but a vehicle to help you through life, while looking to help other people. If you bless others - you will be blessed!

Money is but an element of life. That's why I waited until chapter 8. That's because money is consuming and distorting people. It's breaking up marriages, tainting politics, and producing evil. My words too are with a full understanding of how money tricks people. So the responsibility of money is as important as acquiring money itself.

With that said, I love my people. We are some money getters for real! We refuse to lose and I respect that. But we have to do better with our money. We must set better examples for future generations! We show them how to dress, but don't tell them how to acquire a business.

I come from a large family. As I stated earlier in the book, my grandparents had 15 children. Out of those 15 children and all of the many descendants, only one of them have a business. Just one! How is that possibly out of hundreds of people? Do you know why it's like that? Because we don't teach each other.

I'm calling for African Americans to stop fakin and get on top of their finances. Do not live for the moment, live to gain momentum. Why would you want to live a whole life without leaving a legacy? Our legacy is left arguing over who will pay for the funeral. That's not right!

The most important principle of money is learning how it works. Once you learn how it works, you will begin to make it work for you. But for the life of you, PLEASE don't keep wasting it on swag. I just said swag, and personally I despise the word.

How do you turn on swag? You either are or you're not! But this is what we feed each other.

Trump has HUGE plans in the works! This is for all people whether white, black, Spanish, Asian, you name it - get on point! The Republicans got the presidency, Congress, and Senate. That money is moving and you better be prepared to move with it! Get on point with your savings and investments. There's no time to waste on fear and procrastination. Jump in the game and create better for your families. Sacrifice is vital to financial growth. The number 1 principle being to save. You don't save to say you're saving. You don't save for the sake of saving. You save to give yourself options. Options create opportunity!

The title of this chapter is *"Rich Friends - Poor Enemies"* That is a truth that hovers over social circles. When the rich man speaks, everybody is attentive. When he delivers a joke, the listeners over laugh. The rich man has many friends. Life is not so kind to the poor man. His jokes are rarely laughed at. His love has to fill the void of limited money. His enemies are unconventional in stature. The insurance company, landlord, and cell phone company. His lack of resources to handle his bills on time, becomes his enemies. Unlike the rich man, the poor encounters far more pressure.

The best thing you can do for your children is explain money to them. I'm not talking about counting quarters and dimes.

Let them know about credit, taxes, and saving. The information as I said earlier, has to be available to children.

My mother and father never talked to me about saving. Save what? My mother worked hard to take care of us, there wasn't nothing to save, let alone talk about it. I learned to save through blowing money. I was well into my 30's before I applied the principles of saving seriously. Now, my wife and I know the importance of saving and staying aware of our progress with it.

We all look at money differently. A $1,000 to you, may not hold the same value to someone else. Our occupations and circumstances vary. One thing I pray we agree on, is the eradication of poverty. Too many families in America are struggling from meal to meal. This is a serious problem for humanity. The playing field is not level. Some people will die in debt. If only they had the information and resources.

A select group of billionaires have begun a quest to give away a large majority of their wealth. Warren Buffet, Michael Bloomberg, Mark Zuckerberg, along with Bill and Melinda Gates. They are giving to charities with merit that are specifically handling issues that are important to them. My respect to them and all the many others who donate time and money to organizations. One person cannot change the enormity of poverty, but many of us joined together can. First step - get out of self!

Selfishness is a by - product of the self-society. Why do you think so many people are in love with selfies? We all for self! Me- Me - Me - Me - Me. That's why the money is failing to circulate. Too many *me's*!

This book is not big enough for me to express all of my views and opinions. I am only able to sketch my feelings on subjects. When I conceived the idea of a chapter on money, so many things came to mind.

Now, that I'm here my feelings have been tempered. I say that because a lot of me was angry about poverty. I carried that pain on my sleeve because of my ties to it. Now I realize that there's no place for anger. All I can do is give you my views and hope it inspires you.

The other day while speaking to my wife, she said something humorous. Although it was funny, it still held a lot of meaning. I'm telling her about where I'm at in the book, and she's half sleep while I'm talking. She then says half sleep, "write my money." Write her money? I know she was being funny, but it inspired me. So the running joke now is me saying, "I'm busy writing your money!" Inspiration can come from anywhere - even humor!

Do not be afraid! Step out on faith. If you have an idea, put it in motion. Nothing beats a failure but a try. You can do anything you put your mind to. The thought of a business, a book, a venture, can seem unrealistic. It's not! All I did was grab something I could write on. What can you grab to start an idea? Write your plan down and make it plain. Always do something to advance your plan.

If ever there was a collision of rich and poor, it was this pass election cycle. The billionaire Donald Trump speaking to the downtrodden amongst us. Pumping his fists and saying he feels our pain. The hat, the candor, and the regularity, yet he is still a billionaire.

To many Americans, he was Robin Hood coming back to save us from the evil political establishment. The honeymoon was great until the budget proposal came out cutting spending to the neediest departments for the people. Rich dad wins again.

We are all in this together. The poverty in our country is nobody's burden. There were many factors involved in getting us to this point. A point where our inner cities infrastructure is ravaged. Healthcare is still too high. The equal share of wealth availability is a joke! You want the facts, I'm giving you the facts! The facts of poverty run from the inner cities to rural America.

I think a lot about the children growing up inside poverty's belly. The obstacles they will face. To be born into something with no choice in the matter. For it to feel normal. The new social war we're facing is not about race. This war is about class. The pain of my words will not provide a miracle cure. But if you are reading this, I pray it inspires you.

The opportunity is there. The opportunity to teach a child the principles of money. The opportunity is for you to save and stop wasting money on materials. To learn about stocks and small business. To gain financial independence.

The information is there. The same way we Google a co-workers name, or interesting food we saw; we can find interest in bonds, mutual funds, and land ownership. The world is undergoing a financial cosmetic surgery. Programs are being cut; classes are being defined. I'm putting you on point now!

Be ahead of the game. Discipline will be your closest ally. Greed will be your definitive enemy.

Please remember what I said - don't be afraid. Fortune goes to the bold! I am not a financial expert or Wall Street tycoon. I am just like you. Just trying to make good choices with money that can one day help my family. Nobody really asks for the poor dad. Until next time - think and grow rich!

Quote me....

We must believe the things we tell our children.

- Woodrow Wilson

9

More Truth

President Trump fires F.B.I. director James Comey. This comes after weeks in which director Comey, confirmed possible collusion between members of the Trump administration and the Russians. The same Comey that very well may have helped President Trump win the presidency, by leaking information regarding the investigation into Hillary Clintons emails just days before the election. You're fired! I guess we forgot about Trump, the reality T.V. show host on the apprentice. But seriously, how do you fire the person investigating you, during the investigation? This is so sad, that it's almost becoming comical.

Today is May 4th 2017. To be alive at this moment in history is a gift. But in so many ways it's a curse. I'm pretty sure you share my sentiments on that. I love my family and the possibilities of life. On the other hand, I struggle with the world and its' destructive ways.

Today's breaking news, interrupted Wendy Williams gossip time. It was a briefing on the new healthcare act that passed through congress by a narrow margin. The voting breakdown was 217 yays and 212 nays. This being the same healthcare bill that failed just weeks ago. Apparently a few changes were made and President Trump made some influential calls. Good old politics!

This is why I told how vital the midterm elections were. Those congressmen and senators that you rarely pay attention to, are shaping our world in so many ways. Please pay attention to the lessons right in front of you. They did a drastic healthcare bill today right under your nose, and you had no say in the matter. Breaking news the only indicator.

George Stephenopolous commented several times that quite a number of congressmen voted in the blind, not even knowing what revisions were made.

How disrespectful to the American people. To rush a healthcare bill to vote, that just weeks ago was shot down! To make a few changes, and bring it right back is hoodwinking at its finest! They called it a victory. How petty of them.

President Trump held a news conference in the rose garden. Behind him as he spoke, a wall of republicans standing tall and smiling bright. The slogan was, "Death to Obamacare!" Amongst the fifty or so Republican faces in the rose garden, not a single one of color. Not an Asian, Hispanic, African American, nothing! It was a quiet shot of undertones aired right at President Obama. This is your America.......

The lack of diversity in the Republican Party is not my central issue. We all know that republicans are traditionally a non-inclusive party. OK - I'll suck that up! What really pisses me off, is the rush to push a healthcare bill. A bill that will affect hundreds of millions of Americans. Is it not worth the necessary time to get it right?

The early projections of the plan has up to 34 million Americans losing healthcare; and another uncountable number of Americans on Medicaid becoming uninsured. Oh, let me not forget, there's a HUGE tax cut included for the rich. Why would President Trump do anything without his rich friends benefiting?

Are you still with me? Have you been paying attention to me for 9 chapters? Or were you busy judging me because I use to sell drugs? It's not about me - it's about the future! I am a human being who's made mistakes in life. That does not mean I don't care! You will not find a more honest reporter of what our world is right now. It's never personal- it's just business!

I have no allegiance to anyone but my wife and family. My voice can't be bought. I rejected cursing in this book, as to not offend anyone. My wife's idea totally. I wanted to cuss because of all the frustration inside of me, even though I'm not curser! Sometimes, life makes you wanna let it out!

Have you ever wanted something so bad that it pulls on your soul? It's like a constant bite nipping at your heart. You eat, sleep, and dream it! No matter where you are - work, home, in the shower etc........ it's there. Some people call it passion, and others call it your calling.

For the Bible says "many are called, but few are chosen." Many of us hear that voice inside us saying, "you need to do this." Some begin to pursue that direction immediately, while others pretend not to hear the voice. I believe in my heart that all of us hear that voice at one point in life. Acting on it is the hard part.

Bill Gates was born to navigate technology's growth. Beyonce' was born to sing, dance, and entertain.

Albert Einstein was born to push the laws of physics. Being born to do something is different than being called or chosen to do it.

I've always felt called to do great things. To be a light to people! To love and inspire. Even with that feeling inside of me, I've still felt failure knocking at my door. The fear creeps in and tries to take hold of you. "Don't write that book- nobody's gonna read it anyway." You know what I'm talking about don't you? It's the constant presence of fear. Fear is meant to cripple your drive.

As I type this to you, I feel stronger than I've ever felt before. I'm confident. I know it's because I'm doing something right! When you are doing something right it gives you an inner strength. Like you know you can do it! Writing you these 9 chapters has been healing to me. It has given me a place to unveil my voice. To be heard. Because I'm really concerned for future generations.

I am worried about the state of our education system. Are our children learning enough to compete with an ever changing world? Do they have the proper education to move our country into the next realm of possibility?

I speak on the pain that holds the souls of those stuck in the cold. I speak on the pain of the people. The mothers who had to bury their sons. The wives who wait up all night for their husbands.

The children who are never told, "I love you." The pain of the people has been told between the lines of my words. My punctuation expertise nowhere near the exemplary standards set by Aristophanes Greek perfection. Yet in my own error, I speak the peoples' pain.

To say President Donald Trump is a narcissist does it no justice. Here is a man so protective of his ego, he refused to attend the White House correspondents' dinner. The war on the media betrothed by President Trump is a slap in the face of American democracy.

People are still outraged. Preferring to call him #45 instead of President Trump. This distaste will most likely last until November 2020. On that day you will have the biggest voter turnout in American history. I predict that minorities will play the biggest role in the next election.

No charges will be filed against the officers who shot and killed Alton Sterling. An officer turned himself in this morning after opening fire on a car of teenagers and killing a 15 year old black boy. The Charleston, South Carolina officer who shot Walter Scott in the back, appears to be close to getting off! I'm really not in the mood to explain locations, dates, shooting scenarios, and probabilities. Enough of that has been done for years to no avail. People are still dying at the hands of police officers.

My uncle Jeff was shot in the head by Prince George's county police when I was a child. He was accused of stealing out of Landover Mall. All I remember hearing is something about him running away and the officer shooting him. The same way that Walter Scott was running away. The backing away retreat that Mike Brown attempted. The 300 plus pound Eric Gardener submitting to police officers demands, and still being choked to death. Humbly saying "I can't breathe - I can't breathe."

It appears to me that I can't stay away from topics oppressive to the American race. That's probably why I won't receive that Pulitzer.

People would much rather read fiction or fantasy, instead of all this real life chaos and drama. I have no choice! I promised myself when starting the small book that it would be direct. No wasted words. No more than 9 or 10 chapters. My time is running out!

There will be no closing or extra space dedicated to me for gloating on my writing exploits. I don't deserve it. I'm unsure if this is even good enough to be read. Will I be a failure if nobody likes it? My wife says while editing it, "baby its good! There's nothing like this out there."

A wife is supposed to say that. Oh well, time is running out, and there's some things I really need to say.......

Invest in our children PLEASE! Pay attention to them. Motivate and them. If you tell them something long enough, they'll begin to believe it. The pressures on teenagers is back like the 90's. Teens are more aggressive and more disconnected.

In the 90's teenagers were labeled super predators. This was for violent teens who committed violent acts that gave them life sentences without parole. We're talking about 15, 16, 17 year old kids. They were to be casted away to die behind barbwire fences and castrated dreams.

The Supreme Court ruled in 2014 that those sentences were unconstitutional because a teenagers' brain had not fully developed to make rational decisions. Nearly 2,000 so called "super predator teens" were ordered to receive parole hearings or other remedies to the sentences. Many have since been released since the 2014 ruling, and are living productive lives.

This instance is but one problem plaguing our Justice system.

The United States has the highest rate of incarceration in the world. It's a big business, and a lot of people are cashing in! Many are serving ridiculously long sentences for crimes committed as young adults or teens. Men and women lost inside an unforgiveable system. The families left to carry the burdens of "what ifs" and hopes left unfulfilled. Have you ever REALLY looked into your justice system? They take your tax dollars to fund it - might as well know what the money is being spent on.

I am not going to sit here and pretend that some people don't deserve incarceration. Violent crimes are never acceptable, and I send my sincerest sympathies to anyone who has been a victim of violence, or that knows someone who was. It's wrong and inexcusable! My concern is redemption for those of us who make mistakes or errors in judgement.

My question to you is this....... How much punishment is enough? If a person serves 25 to 30 years for a crime committed in their 20's, is that enough punishment? This person is now in their late 40's or 50's. Will they go back into society and commit a similar offense as to the one committed in their 20's. Here's a better question..... Will they ever commit another offense in his or her lifetime? That's something to think about!

The state of Virginia, abolished parole in the get tough on crime 90's. Which commands men and women to serve at least 85% of a sentence. I say 85% because you have to earn even that with exemplary behavior.

This stark reality for Virginia prisoners prompted Governor Terry McAuliffe to appoint a bi-partisan parole commission to investigate the effects of Governor George Allen's abolishment of parole law in 1995.

Dialogue took place, but no concrete changes to the law. Sometimes perception interferes with the prospect of change. So for now, Virginia prisoners, and other prisoners across The United States, have long sentences to serve. This all boils down to one very simple theory..... Do people deserve second chances? If so, than how does the justice system provide that? I am not trying to persuade your inner conscience, just putting light on an unspoken issue. An American issue. Let's move on....

With the book quickly approaching a close, I turn to you. How are you? How do you feel spiritually, mentally, physically, emotionally? When's the last time you checked these four indicators of your wellbeing? Always take time to check on yourself. If you're not okay - how can you make sure anybody else is okay? Be gentle to yourself? It's almost impossible to please everyone in your life - so don't try! Do your best with the relationships you covet. After you do your best as a mother, father, son, daughter, friend, employee, etc.......please rest! The many hats we wear in life, make perfection in all these areas impossible. Prioritize and be accountable to those things. I pray all is well with you and those you love. Thank you for going on this journey with me.

Although this is a small book, it feels like a lot came out of me. I had no intentions of sharing that much of my life with you, but it came out naturally. The funny thing is I only scratched the surface.

My life has so many folds and creases, as I'm sure yours does also.

My truth leads me to believe in certain formalities. That we all are different. Seeing life in pastel colors and strange shapes. Each color and shape unique in its own way. President Trump is seeing life in hues that 95% of us will never get the chance to see. As he sits in position, as the most powerful man of the free world, a hotel blocks away from the White House bears his name. This is what democracy gave us.

Humanity has been tricked! Tricked by politics, technology, entertainment, sports, and social pressures. We see ourselves so much in selfies, that we don't recognize the unseen anymore. Even if that person sleeps under the same roof as us.

Our sensationalism with all this fickle, has trickled down into our most secure halls of life. That same fickleness gave us Trump. Now reality has set in. Life is so...... you know.

The other day as my wife spoke to my grandson about the book, he pondered on the title. He asked, "grandma, life is so.… what?" My wife looked at him and said, "life is so what? - you tell me." My grandson looked at her and said, "life is so unfair." The nerve of a 7 year old having the audacity to speak such venom. Surely his school work, friends and video games, should shield him from life's rigors.- Obviously not!

Right now in Jackson Mississippi, a federal appeals court is hearing arguments about a Mississippi law that will allow merchants and government employees, to cite religious beliefs to deny services to the L.G.B.T. community. Once again hate is being covered up by the first amendment religious rights guaranty.

What freedom should the L.G.B.T. person have?

We hide behind these same American freedoms that give us freedoms. People do have the right to be against gay marriage. But to provoke hate against them and infringe on their rights is wrong!

My mind elevates into parallels not yet approached. Feeling life's movements with every beat of my heart. Seeing truth while others pretend to be sleep. Fearless of truths consequences.

I feel an enormous responsibility to so many! My immediate and extended family. Our children are having children now. Hopefully I've made them proud. My wife and I want to set an example so bad. To be called...... To be chosen..... To leave a legacy that impacts people.... PRICELESS!!!

In other news, my girl Whoopi was on the view Friday, going at Trump and the republicans. You know the hot topic - that rushed healthcare bill. And just as I suspected, many of the Republicans voted on the bill without reading it. The nerve! There's no respect for us, just political posturing to accomplish their objectives. Whoopi went right at them and I salute her.

Many Republicans were greeted at their local offices by very unhappy constituents. Which serves them right for playing politics with peoples' healthcare. The plot thickens for crucial elections in November. If you've taken nothing else away from this book, take away the importance of your voice. You have the right to speak on the he issues affecting your life. Start speaking!

As for race, it seems good sometimes and then it just goes bad.

The latest incident last week occurred at American University in our Nation's Capital...... Bananas were hung on a tree, with the letters AKA wrote on them. The letters AKA in reference to the African American women's sorority Alpha Kappa Alpha on campus. The leader of the fraternity was later threatened on social media. She currently is being provided around the clock protection by campus security.

This is our 2017 and it's real! A young women goes to college to get an education. She joins a fraternity and rises through the ranks to represent said fraternity. Then one day she and the fraternity are targeted by racist actions. What did she do wrong? Is her only mistake in life, the mathematical odds of being born Black? I thought colors only mattered as kids, picking through Crayola boxes. I guess I was wrong!

As for me.. .. I'm here with you. This has been the hardest challenge of my life. To speak from my heart without any fear of ridicule or judgement. To speak to you without the impulse to impress you or want you to like me. To be he educated man that I am, while holding true to the street instincts I learned as a child. To represent my wife, children, grandchildren and family with grace. To tell the truth! But most importantly, to relay the words directly to you, given to me by God. I am not smart or wise enough to complete a project like this. God is in control.

What would be the best outcome for me with this small book???? It would be for you to see life in a different perspective. Take race, class, and positioning out of it. Void the allure of Twitter and Instagram. Resist your urges to criticize, judge, or downgrade. Destroy your prejudices. Just see life as a human being for a second. The clarity will shock you!

I hope I served you well. I know I was hard on politicians and racists, but they left me no choice! People aren't being treated fairly. To the good upstanding politicians - I say thank you. We need you to right the wrongs of your fellow politician. Don't turn the blind eye to their misdeeds and mischief. Time is closing in on all the antics and side bars. The American people are waking up! The protests are happening more frequently. Enough is almost enough!

Protect our children and love our women. If you know commitment is not for you, don't tell her you want a relationship. I pray for my daughters' every day, that good men will come into their lives. Women you have got to be accountable also. You can't say "respect me," and behave loose and reckless. If all you know is twerking, then you will attract twerk liking guys.

Let me close the only way I can......God is so awesome! I told you parts of my life. I was a lost young man. All of those nights, I could of been killed. God spared me and gave me a gift. That gift is love. I am thankful.

Life is so.... you know.

10

One Small Bonus Chapter

Dropping my keyboard has been the hardest thing to do. It seems like each week comes bombarded with more breaking news that cannot be ignored. As soon as I tell my wife I'm done, CNN turns me into a liar! So here I go with this small bonus chapter hoping that you're still on point. Fighting for inches as you can see.

These words will be the REALEST of the book, so please hold on to your seat......,,

A special salute to martyr Heather Heyer, who died tragically in Charlottesville this weekend. A mob of Nazi, KKK, alt right members, spurned the innocent streets of Charlottesville with hate. The hate was on full display, followed by vicious rounds of violence.

The excuse??? Those damn Confederate statues again! The statues have become the quickest way to divulge hate.

Heather Heyer and two state troopers died. The crowd was about 80% caucasian, which I found to be astonishing! The white race, fighting the white race, for all races- AMAZING!!! Then for it to be in Virginia, the very state where slavery started, brings the course of oppression circle.. The very state that founded slavery, is now y protected by white people for ALL PEOPLE.

The optics of the whole incident truly touched my heart. This was not about black, white, rich, or poor, this was about good versus evil! Our world is truly changing....

#45 took flack from both sides of the aisle, for not calling out the white supremacy, KKK, as hate groups. He called out everybody else! (women, Muslims, Mexicans, Hillary, John McCain, Obama, gangs etc... etc... etc...)

Then he had the nerve to try and clean it up today. Too late for many, but needed relief for others.

Let me stand for truth and love right now....

We should not have to tell our president to call out hate groups. We should not accept hate in any form. Our president (#45), should staunchly detest these acts without coaxing. The movement has started and you have to choose: What side you're on! Remaining silent is a travesty.

So much for my small book dream. This book will still be a little over 100 pages or so. But how could I ignore so many crucial issues in our world? To quote the words of Heather Danielle Heyer, " If you are not outraged, you are not paying attention!" I've been telling y'all that since I started the book. WAKE UP!!!!

Here's what we're gonna do.... We are gonna unite and stand taller than ever! We are gonna speak out and PEACEFULLY protest. Heather Heyers mother has asked that we not let her daughters death be in vain. Don't be afraid- be inspired! There's more love in the world than hate. Just do your part.

Now, let's go back to those statues for a moment. Mayors from Richmond, Baltimore, Birmingham, and many other cities are calling for the removal of the Confederate statues. Some mayors have ordered them removed by executive actions. In some cases, their being destroyed by citizens who are doing what they feel is right. Are we allowing statues to perpetuate and incite hate?

What are the statues up for anyway? These men committed treason. They ignored the law enacted by President Lincoln freeing the slaves. How is fighting for the right to own a human is honorable? BE FOR REAL!!! People say it's Confederate pride. Pride in what? Keeping slaves in bondage? How does that deserve a monument?

We have a clear representation of something (confederate statues), that has invoked so much pain in so many people, yet it's celebrated. Why would a portion of our country be so callous? All history is not good history, and I wish we would stop hiding behind it.

I know I've said a lot, and hopefully I won't regret it one day. If I do, I guess I can hide under my freedom of speech clause. Hopefully my words showed you life in a different light. What's up with that Pulitzer? As I said, from the beginning, if the book was ever privileged enough to win an award, I would donate it. I would find the most down trodden elementary school in the country, and give those kids a reason to dream.

Alright, I'm signing off for real now. Shout to Sweets, Velli, Ma, Diane, Eric, R.F., Author House publishing, Dr. Nelson (seriously), Governor McCauliff, and anyone else who inspired this work. Thanks to my P.G., D.C., Mpls, Okc, N.C.,and Baltimore family. To all the souljahs behind the fence, stay encouraged! I'm dropping my mic.......................

Hello again...... I'm kind of back by default. This one small chapter was somehow left out the original copy of the book. After much thought and careful consideration, I decided it has to be in here! I just feel bad for those who have already bought the book, who may not even know this 1 small chapter exists. It also cost me a pretty penny to get the resubmittance specialist to add it, but what wouldn't I do for my readers

Since I'm here and I paid the fee I might as well bring you up to speed on now...... The shootings in Las Vegas and Texas were devastating! To think that we are no longer safe at a music venue or church is troubling. Now you see why I went at the N.R.A. the way I did in the book. There has to be more detailed screening for gun buyers, especially where mental health is involved. My heart and prayers go out to the victims loved ones.

#45 is still leaving a trail of misunderstanding wherever he goes. Just last night he was trading insults (on twitter), with Kim Jong like two middle schoolers. Maybe his is what the reality t.v. phenomenon gave us!

The republicans are pushing another tax reform bill with all perks for the rich. Special note to republicans: There are more middle and lower class Americans than rich Americans. I know you want to cater to corporations and businesses, but we are the ones who support those entities.

The Democrats stomped last weeks election. There was also historic changes in race, gender, and even transgender incumbants. Some have called it a referendum against #45. I say it's people tired of the same old same old. #45 might turn out to be a gift in disguise at next years mid terms.

Indictments were handed down by special investigator Mueller in the Russian collision investigation. Are you shocked? I'm not! They been stealing money and making deals under the table for years. This is only the beginning, wait until ALL the dirt comes out.

As for me, just working hard on promoting this book and working on the next one. The Father, Lover, and Hustler will be coming at you this spring. NOTHING like this has ever been printed! Please tell a friend to tell a friend to support Life is so you know. People need to hear this.

Other than that, my best to you. Stay on point, and I will be back in your ear soon!

Closing: Life is moving fast

I've contemplated a closing for weeks now. I even told my wife that I've probably said enough. I've flirted with a tribute letter to my wife, that didn't go over too well with her. She said it was too personal, and gave up too much tea. I guess I took the whole being truthful thing literally. A part of me just wanted to give her some shine for all that she does. Because none of this happens without her. So I guess I can give her some shine right now by saying, "baby I thank you and love you beyond." How can words ever be enough?

Since I got a minute, I might as well put my readers up on game...... The Washington Post is reporting that Jared Kushner tried to set up a secret and secure communication channel between Donald Trumps transition team, and the Kremlin. Mr. Kushner requested to use Russia's diplomatic facilities. Russian Ambassador Sergey Kislyak reportedly was taken aback by the mere suggestion of allowing an American to use Russian gear at its embassy or consulate. I guess Trumps son in-law had a lot to talk about!

So lets add up the points to collusion.....

Trump publicly praises Putin on several occasions. Trumps former campaign manager Paul Manafort, has major money ties to Russia. Trumps Secretary of State Rex Tillerson, received a friendship award from Russia. Then you got Michael Flynn, who was Trumps first national security advisor, with so much Russia in his portfolio, that he was forced to resign. (Flynn even looks sneaky) Add in Trump firing F.B.I. director James Comey, who was in charge of the Russian investigation, and it all smells funny. It actually smells a little watergatish to me. Or here goes one.... If it walks and quacks- we got a duck!

Some naive Americans are probably saying, "what's the big deal with Russia?" The big deal is, Russia is very deceptive. The big deal is, Russia has a history of espionage and plots against America. The big deal is, Russia is strapped with hackers, organized crime syndicates, and billionaires. I think we all know what money tends to do to politicians. Why else would Ru$$ia be so popular now. Greed has a way of making complexed situations appear innocent. Just ask President Trump..........

Since my last words to you in chapter 9, police officers across America are still abusing citizens. People are more outraged by the new healthcare act, and Trumps proposed budget. The budget cutbacks will be devastating to countless American families. The common excuse is, "too many people are taking advantage of government handouts". Alright, I agree that some people are taking advantage of government assistance..... But what about those who are not? What about those family's that cling to survival by food stamps and other services? Do we punish the majority that needs the help, for the minority that abuses the aid? That seems like a no brainer to me - you help people!

American politicians act like American politicians are not the blame for many of Americas problems. Nobody wants to be poor. Who wants to enter a grocery store, shop for food, and then pull out a food stamp card when the cashier asks for payment? Nobody wants that exposure.

But this is what our America gave us. Our very founding of freedom was flawed. The document states, "We hold these truths to be self-evident, that all men are created equal. That they are endowed by their creator, with certain inalienable rights. That among these are life, liberty, and the pursuit of happiness." How could such profound and eloquent words be flawed? Let me explain.......

Our founding fathers were in conflict as these words were written. Thomas Jefferson, James Adams, and Benjamin Franklin, were all slave owners. So for them to collaborate and etch such words, while still in self conflict with its tone, immediately errors the document. This observation is in no way a slight at our founding fathers for having the courage to create such a document. I am even sure that many of them even questioned their own roles in slavery, in introspective views.

I am not slamming them for decisions they may have thought were correct. The first ship of slaves were docked on the shores of Jamestown Virginia in 1619. So Jefferson, Adams, and Franklin were only continuing an ugly truth that was 150 plus years old, by time their moment in history was upon us. Which makes it all relative to today's America.

Many people are not being treated fairly today. Minorities, women, poor folks, Muslims, and sexually different people as well. That same document should be a protector for them. But the Life, Liberty, and Pursuit of happiness is flailing at best. People dispute who should be treated fairly. Who should have the right to these provisions? When our forefather's stated that, "they are endowed by their creator, with certain inalienable rights". So they made the whole matter of rights bigger than them. They granted that guarantee to God our creator. So why don't we follow the standard of this document? Because honestly, it's just a document!

So I ask humbly...... Can a proceeding document be made that offers inclusion? Can a document be made for women, minorities, immigrants, and sexually different Americans? Can a document be made for who we are today? This is no disrespect to our Declaration, but our world is different now. We can now see each other on phones while we talk. Drones are roaming the air!

I'm sure author Thomas Jefferson won't mind some revisions. The same Thomas Jefferson who fathered several children with a slave hand named Sally. My point is, our founding was not perfect! So why can't some of our brightest minds, congregate in a undisclosed location, and deliver a document of inclusion for the American people? Would that be un-American? I believe it would inflict healing.

Let's look at the Emancipation Proclamation for a second..... This was a document that declared all slaves free in 1863. But what exactly did this freedom mean?

Were slaves free from bondage? Free from labor and chattel service? What were the slaves free from? Obviously something went wrong, for there to be colored only signs on bathrooms in the 1960's. What happened to that document that freed the slaves in 1863? Maybe it was just a document.

I challenge you right now, to ask for more from your world. I challenge you to rise up and speak on equal pay for women. Susan B. Anthony is probably turning in her grave, witnessing the lack of fight by some over women's issues. I ask that you fight against the continued systemic imprisonment of African Americans. We all know that our justice system is the most flawed entity in our nation. I challenge you to ensure that ALL of our God given rights, are furbished to ALL classes, races, and genders. For the rights of a middle class white man, should be equal with that of a lower class transgender American. Our founding fathers said that our creator endows us with these inalienable rights. I challenge you to look beyond preference and conformity.

Life is moving fast! Every day there's a new headline to digest. Kathy Griffith made an insensitive joke about president Trump, and people are calling for an end to her career. A man in Mississippi snaps and kills 8 people. A mother in Tucson, abandons her daughter to pursue a Facebook relationship. Fear of what's next, is a scary reality.......

Time is moving fast. It's so easy to become overwhelmed! Don't buy into the propaganda. Life will move at the pace you set. One thing that slows life down, is concern for others. When you do what's right, time intentionally slows down to let you relish the moment. As a matter a fact, time right now has slowed to a snails pace. I feel that God has given me this designed moment to share this hope with you. I am not intrigued by my own life or surroundings there of. My heart rests in the hopes of better for mankind. That's what this book was about. Life is so……… you know. I gave my opinion, and you will have your own. But at least we are thinking about it.

For now, pay attention to your world. We have a President in Washington entranced in scandal and perplexity. We have a dictator in North Korea begging to go to war. A culture more intrigued with social media, than the senseless murders inside of our inner cities. Why should people have to remind us that black lives matter? Can you hear me crying out to you? I know that life is moving fast, and the sound of voices are elusive. Just slow things down, and you will hear things clearly Can you hear the marching of the LGBT community pleading for rights? Can you hear the silent cries of the victims in Charlottesville? Can you hear the confusion of our children? Can you hear the silent prayers from mother's in the middle of the night? Can you hear the whimpering of slaves from the days gone by? Can you hear the pleads for help from women being physically abused? Can you hear the innocence of our children being betrayed for pleasure?

I can rest now…… I've said the things my heart encouraged me to say. My wife and I, will now prepare this for publishing. Hoping that it's supported and accepted. Praying that a voice like mine is needed. I may even start a sequel, just in case you want to hear more. But for now, I'll keep my ear to the ground for you. Slowing life down enough to hear what's necessary. So I ask you to fill in the blank…… Life is so_____?

Deon H. 17'

The world is really moving fast. Collusion is everywhere! Trump's son has talked to the Russians, Trump's son in law has talked to the Russians, and most of Trump's friends has talked to the Russians. If you are not awake, you better hurry up. Grab a cup of Folgers, and tune in. The Russians took our election and you are obsessed with seeking perfection. Somebody is lying! Trump is pointing the finger at

Comey, and Comey is pointing the finger at Trump. So here are the facts.......

Either your President is lying, or your ex FBI director is lying. Take your pick, but know that you are being lied to. If you are not woke yet, maybe you should just keep sleeping. Goodnight.

Excerpt from next book: The Father, Lover and Hustler

Dukes Poetry.....

I was stupid enough to fly to Oregon to grab a birds eye view of the eclipse last August. I guess that's why we hustle, to enjoy the moments of life! Whether your hustle is postal deliverer, man of purpose, woman who is a boss, or even a web designer. See those moments and savor them. Life is all about chasing eclipses and tickets front row for Lionel Richie. Well, that is what I look forward to. Those are solidify family bonds. They endear you to your wife and make you a hero to your kids. Of course you didn't think I flew to Oregan alone chasing eclipses by myself.

My wife and kids fly how I fly. We invest in moments that will yield a profit from said investments. I invest in people I love and see every day. He greatest investment being time. Most people will say, "love." But that's not true for the following reasons.... (Pay Attention)

1. *God gives each of us a blue printed amount of TIME to love.*
2. *Love is unattainable, without the necessary amount of time to receive it or reciprocate it.*
3. *Love takes TIME "heard that before?"*

Anyways, we will have plenty of time to speak on time. Hustling, investing and progression with your family / finances. I can see my mother now, advising me on writing techniques after reading this book thoroughly. "Duke, you could have sounded a little more Warren Buffet on chapter so and so." Then I'll say, "I feel you ma, but it's an in trospect in literature from three separate individuals. This is also a candid look into each of our lives." Then I'll get real jovial and say, "I'm writing as the hustler and I can talk turkey with the best of them!" For now, I will give them just enough to come back......

Three intoxicatingly likable people who share their joys, pain, triumps and trials in life. It's bitter truth and sad realities. You will definitely relate to one of them if not all. Movie worthy.

Printed in the United States
By Bookmasters